To Jody and the family,

It has been a pleasure and a privilege working on your wine country book. I'm looking forward to the book signing parties!

xo Chase

At Home in the
Wine Country

At Home in the Wine Country

ARCHITECTURE & DESIGN IN THE CALIFORNIA VINEYARDS

Heather Sandy Hebert
and Chase Reynolds Ewald

GIBBS SMITH
TO ENRICH AND INSPIRE HUMANKIND

Contents

WINE COUNTRY CONTEMPORARY

RECREATION & RENEWAL

Introduction

The California wine country is a region without distinct edges, which seems only appropriate given its global influence. From the northern tip of San Francisco Bay up the length of the Napa Valley and beyond, arcing over to the Russian River Valley to the fog-draped coastal Sonoma hills, then down the coast to the Carmel Valley and continuing south to Santa Barbara County, California's wine country eschews definition as it continues to expand and evolve.

In recent decades, the region has come to be defined by its lifestyle as much as its wines. It has developed its own ethos, one whose contemporary expression is creative, sustainability minded, art-filled and bathed in light. Highly refined yet without pretense, it has a youthful attitude and a decided sense of fun. Central to California living is the indoor-outdoor experience; today's homes seamlessly integrate the region's sublime scenery and climate with its cuisine and lifestyle.

Each in our own way, we were destined to explore it. Heather was raised within the architecture community of Northern California, and went on to craft a career focused on translating the magic of architecture and design into words, both as the longtime marketing director for an international architecture practice and as a freelance writer. Chase came to the West Coast as a graduate student, in part to discover her fourth-generation California roots, and stayed to document the history, design, cuisine and art of the American West.

When we met, we were both at work on books exploring different facets of the West's vibrant architecture and design community. But one can't live in the Bay Area without encountering a steady stream of wine country news, outings, cultural references and, yes, design. We were both keenly aware of the extent to which wine country architecture had evolved in recent decades, and we were drawn together in our wish to showcase the wine country's unique lifestyle and sense of community. Indeed, as residents of the northern Bay Area, we are part of that community.

Life in the wine country is a unique blending of agriculture and sophistication, lived outdoors amidst surroundings of prodigious beauty. Those drawn to make their home—or second home—in the wine country are often linked to the growing of grapes or the making of wine, but not always. Some simply bring with them a love of wine and the vitality of community it engenders. Indeed, the wine country is a small world, close-knit and supportive, where a pace of life more attuned to the land and seasons allows its residents to form deep bonds. This is a place where new residents rub elbows with families who have cultivated the land for generations.

Nothing has illustrated that spirit more than the response to the fires that have increasingly become a part of the cycle of life in California, burning in the wine country again and again. In each instance, people banded together, supporting one another in a way that only a truly connected community can do, and illustrating for us the resiliency that can come only from a deep connection to the land and its people.

Here, time is measured in seasons, and the notion of renewal is integral to understanding the sense of place. Some vineyards have been in place for over a hundred years, drawing nutrients from roots plunged deep into the sometimes difficult soil. But each year brings new growth, a new crop and new possibilities. So it goes with the people of the wine country, a blending of old and new, sharing an entrenched love of the land and the lifestyle. This likely explains why so many who establish second homes in the wine country tend to spend more and more time here, until the wine country becomes home and their more urban residence becomes a place to visit.

At Home in the Wine Country showcases work from many of the region's top architects and designers. This virtual tour documents a native, terroir-derived style that has evolved dramatically since the days when the region looked to European chateaux for inspiration. The residences featured here comprise just a sample of the extraordinary breadth and depth of work being done today in the wine countries of northern and central California. From refined rustic to updated agrarian to unapologetically modern, the range of styles—as well as the varied approaches to managing environmental factors—is broad. While each project is the result of careful consideration of client, program and site, its starting point is always place.

Set within landscapes of extraordinary beauty, these homes also exist within a fragile environment. Since many dwellings are sited on hillsides within the wildland-urban interface, architects have become well-versed in design principles and practices that minimize impact on the existing environment and increase the structures' resistance to fire. While several homes in our book were threatened by the most recent fires of 2020, all have survived thanks not only to the courage of first responders and community residents, but also to design and building practices that increased their resilience.

Seventeen homes—plus four unique auxiliary structures, including a pool house, a party barn, and a dining pavilion with production gardens—laud wine-country living in an atmosphere of understated, family-focused hospitality.

For one retiree, a sustainable structure with rammed-earth walls within an 18,000-acre eco-development near Carmel is a nature-focused forever home. Further north in Glen Ellen, a simple farmhouse-style weekend retreat represents the culmination of one designer's career interpreting wine-country style as a transplant from the UK. In the hills overlooking Sonoma, a collection of boxes juxtaposes geometric black-and-white forms with disappearing walls against a verdant landscape. Set amid the vines on the floor of the Napa Valley, a cluster of buildings expresses California's agrarian traditions while deftly incorporating a subtle nod to the architectural legacy of the famed Sea Ranch. On a forested hillside, a thoroughly contemporary abode is built as a transparent envelope from which to experience nature, and becomes an expression of the soul of both its place and its owners. A historic bungalow in downtown Sonoma retains its original charm while embracing an exuberantly modern addition for owners of a wine business. Perched on a hillside not far from downtown Napa, a simply rendered house overlooks vineyards with a sweeping view of the valley below, the result of one man's lifelong passion for the work of East Coast icon Hugh Newell Jacobsen.

No work of this type is possible without a legion of architects, interior designers, contractors, landscape architects, engineers, sustainability consultants, lighting designers, art experts, artists and photographers. Without their creativity, passion, institutional knowledge and hard work, projects of this quality would never come to fruition. And none of it would appear in formats like this without homeowners willing to share their most intimate spaces. These are the places to which they retreat to rejuvenate, entertain and make memories, the places in which they can most be themselves. Yet they invite readers in so that these homes—beautiful, unique, responsibly designed and carefully crafted—can be seen, providing us all with pleasure and inspiration.

We couldn't have created this book without their generosity of spirit and their respect for craft, nor could we do what we do without the editors, graphic designers and visionaries at Gibbs Smith Publisher. For that shared vision we are grateful.

At Home in the Wine Country pays homage to a world and a lifestyle that is ever innovating, adapting and evolving. As is often the case with projects like this, the more we explore, the more we find. We are in awe of the talent and artistry assembled within these pages. We're honored to be able to showcase these uniquely sophisticated place-based expressions of home in the wine country.

HEATHER SANDY HEBERT   Chase Reynolds Ewald

Agrarian Spirit

Vineyard's Edge

"In the wine country, every nook and cranny of the land is aesthetically interesting."
— LUKE WADE

Architect Luke Wade says tramping around open land reminds him of his childhood in South Texas, when kids were allowed to disappear for hours or even days on a horse or with a backpack to fish, camp and build forts. Today, he and his wife, Ani Wade, create homes suitable for a wide range of ecosystems and microclimates, from redwood forests to fog-draped cityscapes to sun-drenched properties perched on the side of mountains or surrounded by vineyards on the valley floor. "In the wine country, every nook and cranny of the land is aesthetically interesting," Wade says. "That's what's so amazing about California." It makes sense, then, that every project begins with an exploration of site.

Becoming attuned to site was key to both Wades' professional development; it carries through to everything the pair designs today. They met while working for Backen Gillam Architects. Both became lead designers at the firm, whose name is practically synonymous with California's place-based architecture movement—one that elevates to an art the use of simple forms and natural materials to create unpretentious, timeless structures.

It was this background that initially led Dave and Natalie Hagan to Wade Design. The Hagans, residents of southern California, first visited Napa while on their honeymoon thirty-five years prior. Instantly enamored, they became frequent visitors to the wine country and, in 2005, charter members of Calistoga Ranch. They would visit six times a year, each time exploring hidden byways on the motorcycle they kept there, discovering favorite wines and making friends along the way. Over the course of scores of visits to wineries and private homes, the Hagans fell in love with the look of ag-inspired modern farmhouses and contemporary barns. Then, as they were contemplating buying land and building a home, they visited Constant's Diamond Mountain Vineyard, sited high in the Mayacamas Mountains overlooking northern Napa Valley. The vintners' home, designed by Howard Backen, recalls Dave Hagan, "is very simple, essentially a one-room structure, and very indoor-outdoor, with sliding doors to the outside and phenomenal views. We said, 'This is exactly what we're talking about.'"

Having never lived in a home larger than 2,500 square feet, the Hagans understood their own needs and design preferences and were able to articulate how they lived within an interior; they even wrote up a requirements document for their initial meetings. Each member of the team

they assembled—including contractor Total Concepts, interior designer Lauren Geremia and Ground Studio Landscape Architecture—was open to collaboration and the group meshed seamlessly. The Hagans knew they wanted a human-scaled home, one that would feel intimate when they were in residence as a couple but could easily accommodate their son and houseguests. And they understood that the focus had to be on embracing the extraordinary views of the Mayacamas and Mount St. Helena from their site among the vines on the Napa Valley floor. The result was a main house designed around the primary open living space and open to the outdoors on all sides, a three-suite guesthouse, a small pool house tucked up against mature trees on the far side of the pool, and a two-story barn. This would house a concrete floor garage and workshop and, upstairs, an airy yoga studio with a vaulted and beamed ceiling and big doors on either end to take advantage of the breezes.

The barn is the most visible component and defines the project, explains Luke Wade. In referencing the area's agricultural roots, "The barn anchors the property and makes it right for its place." The structure has a darker hue and a more rustic treatment than the house, as well as a more charismatic presence, but its themes are picked up in the residence, with exterior wood treatment and wood beams repeated in the open-plan living area and bedrooms. The home departs from the rustic, however, in its light, neutral palette within and without and stone floors on a grid that flow from the front door through the house and out onto the terrace. With slim-profile steel windows extending to the floor and flooding the rooms with light, bedrooms whose doors open directly outside, and a roofed and trellised terrace running the length of the structure on the north, one is immersed in nature at all times.

Interior designer Lauren Geremia helped create a sensibility that would stand the test of time. "In a way," she says, "the house is defined by its doors and windows. Because the floors are the same inside and out and the landscape and color palette flow inside and out, it feels blended into the landscape and really embraces the views. It has a cohesiveness. And it had to have staying power so that the clients would grow into it and love it just as much ten years from now."

Both designer and architects credit Ground Concept's naturalistic approach to the landscaping for linking the components together while integrating into the surroundings, including the vineyard to the north and an equestrian property to the east. The result is a serene retreat that consistently inspires, says the homeowner. "The views are spectacular and the layers of colors—in the palisades, the trees, the grasses, the vineyards—just breathtaking," says Hagan.

"In our first year of retirement," he adds, "we traveled a lot. We did a lot of ten-day trips and went to seven countries. But every time we hit the southern end of the valley we'd say, 'This is just as pretty as anywhere.'"

PREVIOUS OVERLEAF:
Dave and Natalie Hagan had a strong sense of what they wanted for their Napa Valley property. They sought out husband-and-wife architects Luke Wade and Ani Wade and contractor Total Concepts to create a home with a strong sense of place that would take full advantage of spectacular views of the Mayacamas and Mount St. Helena. In a nod to the region's agricultural heritage, a two-story barn, which has a workshop and vehicle storage below and a yoga studio above, anchors the project.

OPPOSITE:
The wood-clad and gabled main house and guesthouse are open to the outdoors on all sides. Bernard Trainor of Ground Studio organized the landscape plan around courtyards and terraces, such as this dining area centered on Piet Hein Eek's zinc table from The Future Perfect. The chairs are from Teak Warehouse.

LEFT:
Designer Lauren Geremia of Geremia Design created interiors with staying power. In the dining area, the Schoolhouse table is from Jeff Martin Joinery, the ladderback dining chairs are Stahl & Band. Tim Kirk Lighting makes the flute pendants, which are hung at different levels.

ABOVE:
An airy sitting area has an in-the-vineyard immediacy. Stone floors on a grid run in, through, and out of the house, unifying the feel and allowing for unimpeded indoor-outdoor flow.

OPPOSITE:
The white Macaubas Quartzite island top, Cloud tile from
Tempest Tileroom, and minimal bar stools from Graye
carry the feeling of serenity through the kitchen. The Grain
Pendants are from Brendan Ravenhill.

ABOVE:
At the entry, guests are greeted by a Kalmar Tulipan
chandelier of blown glass and brass, circa 1950s, and a
painting by Lola "Babe" Atha, who had been a close friend
of Natalie Hagan's parents. The leather-covered banquette
and table were designed by Geremia Design. The CH33T
chairs are by Hans J. Wegner for Carl Hansen; the Open
Meshmatics Pendant is from Atelier Rick Tegelaar.

OVERLEAF:
In the covered outdoor living room, Harbour Outdoor metal
and wood chairs flank a cocktail table from Teak Warehouse.
The integrated benches and fire feature aligned with the
pool allow for cozy moments when the temperatures
drop at night. Ceiling heaters and fans help keep things
comfortable year-round.

Modern Agrarian

"I'm a huge fan of designed places to nap." — MELANIE TURNER

Designed for a family from nearby Marin County and their two teenage children, this house is an oasis of calm—a refuge from the whirlwind of the high tech industry. Though not involved in the wine industry, the family was drawn to the quietude and natural rhythms of the agricultural setting. Introduced to San Francisco-based Pfau Long through the firm's work at their children's school, the owners asked the firm to help them carry out their vision.

Set on the valley floor in the heart of Napa Valley, the 4.2-acre property is surrounded on all sides by vineyards and graced with a mixture of native oaks, redwoods, walnut trees and previously planted palms. Working closely with landscape architects Lutsko Associates on the master plan, the team at Pfau Long devised a cluster of buildings set amid the rural landscape. An early key decision to realign the entry road enables visitors to enter the site through the existing redwood grove, winding through trees until the house and property reveal themselves all at once. A second reveal awaits at the entry, where double-height slatted cedar barn doors slide open to unveil a transparent double-height entry foyer and the full scope of the valley views. In a valley filled with picture-perfect vistas and "wow" moments, this sequence stands apart.

Clad in vertical cedar siding, the main house, adjacent guesthouse, pool house, pottery studio and garage offer a subtle nod to the architectural legacy of the famed Sea Ranch, located on the coast not far away. Using straightforward agricultural forms as their starting point, the architects experimented with framing views and carving out negative spaces, an approach that gives the home a distinctively contemporary feel as it pushes the agrarian aesthetic subtly forward.

"With simple forms, we are always experimenting with carving away, compositionally arranging elements until they feel just right," says Melanie Turner, residential design director at Pfau Long.

This house is surrounded by hundreds of acres of agricultural land, so the natural instinct would be to invite it all in. Instead, the team decided to frame the scenery to create a more intimate relationship to the surrounding vineyards and a very personal relationship to the view.

"When you are outdoors, the vineyards completely surround you, but the interiors provide a different experience, balancing a feeling of safety and refuge within the expansive site. The framed views provide focal points as you move through the interiors," says Melanie.

PREVIOUS OVERLEAF:
Architects Pfau Long and landscape architects Lutsko Associates devised a cluster of buildings set amid a rural landscape that changes with the seasons, creating an oasis of calm for a Marin family.

OPPOSITE:
In the quietly dramatic double-height entry, tall, slatted cedar barn doors slide open to welcome visitors and reveal the full scope of the valley views. Architect Melanie Turner worked with Ralph Dahllof of Grassi & Associates, hand-shaping the elements of the Bocci chandelier to create a truly custom piece.

Like the building forms, the plan is straightforward, composed of two axes with the magnificent double-height entry at the center, while inventive design solutions lend a sense of adventure. A bridge crosses the double-height space, connecting the house's two wings. Oversized ship's wheels, engineered so precisely they can be turned with a single finger, operate the second-floor louvers in the entry foyer. The slatted barn doors provide an ever-changing pattern of light and shadow on the concrete floors, and humble materials such as painted wood siding soften the monolithic space.

Charged with the design of both architecture and interiors, Melanie and her team kept the materials palette to a minimum: primarily cedar, poured concrete, steel and glass. Interior hues are muted and furnishings are minimal but inviting. "We like to keep the textures soft in the areas you touch," says Melanie. The family's dogs are allowed everywhere, so everything needs to be durable. The honest materials, meant to accept a patina over time, keep the ample house from being pretentious.

The design team worked closely with builders Grassi & Associates, highly respected in the valley for their precision-built custom homes. The two firms worked hand-in-hand to craft custom built-in elements and unexpected touches (a very practical "purse nook" in the master bedroom, for example). A favorite story involves the massive glass pendant in the entry foyer: Melanie worked with Grassi's Ralph Dahllof to twist each of the pendant's numerous individual wires to precisely place each of the fixture's dozens of blown-glass globes—a painstaking but ultimately satisfying process.

With generous spaces that flow seamlessly between indoors and outdoors, this home was designed for entertaining. In this temperate valley, where so much of the year can be spent outside, the outdoor spaces are graciously scaled. The home's private spaces, on the other hand, are cozy and enveloping.

The team at Lutsko Associates designed the grounds to provide seasonal explosions of color—yellow, red or lavender—a beautiful and effective way to track the seasons. Continuous site lines—such as stone work on the terraces meticulously laid out to align with the more distant vineyard rows—impart a sense of order and serenity. "The flow from the architecture through to the landscape is one of the strongest aspects of this project," notes Ron Lutsko. Taking advantage of the idyllic setting, these clients live in the landscape, harvesting from the citrus grove, the apple grove and the large, edible garden.

By all accounts, these were dream clients. "They had a very organic and linear process, which shines through in what we were able to achieve with the architecture, and in the ease with which it all came together," says Melanie. Andrea Koval, associate principal at Lutsko Associates, concurs, "There was something that was just so perfect about this team."

ABOVE:
Clad in vertical Port Orford cedar, the structures offer
a subtle nod to the architectural legacy of the famed
Sea Ranch, set on the coast not far away. Soft grasses
coexist with perennials that offer an ever-changing
explosion of color.

OPPOSITE:
Oversized ship's wheels, engineered so precisely they can
be turned with a single finger, operate the second-floor
louvers in the entry foyer.

LEFT:
Architect Melanie Turner worked with the clients to choose
finishes and furnishings that are simple and soothing,
forming a perfect foil for the jaw-dropping valley views
just outside the windows. Rodolfo Dordoni sectional sofas
surround cocktail tables by Belgian craftsman Kaspar
Hamacher.

ABOVE:
In the open-plan kitchen, living and dining areas, concrete
forms the custom countertops, cast-in-place fireplace and
steel-troweled flooring.

OVERLEAF:
A cast-concrete firepit is set below the terrace to form a
natural seating area. Stacked, slatted cedar barn doors slide
open to reveal the transparent double-height entry foyer.

Woodland Farmhouse

"Rossi wanted the house to have the integrity of an old-world farmhouse, from
indigenous Sonoma fieldstone to true board-and-batten siding to hand-troweled stucco."
— DAVID SORENSON

It was the approach that sold him. Despite being located off a busy north-south artery close to Sonoma's historic square, the long, gently meandering lane was pure country. Bordered by grapevines and a horse farm, it was lined with madrone and live oaks whose moss-covered trunks arched over in places to create a tunnel effect. Angus and Rossi Scott had been searching for the perfect country property for five years, and Angus had visited a property on that same access road some years prior. He knew what they were looking for. Which is why, within minutes of the broker telling him about the ten-acre parcel, Angus made a full-price offer, sight unseen.

His instincts served him well. "It's one hour door-to-door from San Francisco with none of the Napa traffic," he says, "and you have a very unspoiled, very historical market town nearby. The road in is lovely, with madrone and oak trees. The land is beautiful, with Mount Diablo clearly visible seventy miles to the east. Rossi grew up in the borders of Scotland and I grew up in the country in England, so we really wanted privacy. You stand on the deck and all you can see is oak trees, vines and the mountains in the distance."

While the purchase happened quickly, the development of the property was a process. Designer Rossi Scott had worked on boats, planes, homes and wineries, but this project necessitated "a readying of the canvas" before they could proceed. They cleared decades of overgrown brush and removed the fencing that crisscrossed the property. A concrete water tank was encased in cedar, retaining walls of local stone were built, and a pool was installed on the flattest, sunniest part of the property. It took two years to bury electrical lines, which were unsightly and a fire hazard.

The Scotts thought their new home would take the form of a barn on the open ground by the pool. But the house, built on stilts in the 1950s and tucked into a treed slope, had the best views and microclimate. And while its layout was good, its condition was not. They started over, with architect Nick Lee taking the lead on structural specifications and Rossi and Lee working together on the design concepts, proportions and space planning for the house, as well as for a barn that would house a garage, party kitchen and bunkroom.

"Rossi had a vision for the property and had already created the setting," explains the architect. "We wanted to keep the spirit of the original house,

OPPOSITE ABOVE:
The serene, light-filled bathrooms benefit from oversized windows and extra-tall doorways. The reclaimed Russian oak vanity with Carrara marble top and Lucent mirror in antique nickel are from RH. The wall-mounted cross-handle faucet is by Kafka UK.

OPPOSITE BELOW:
A quiet corner of the living room is the perfect place to work from home with an oak desk from Waterworks, Swan desk chair in leather and cowhide, cotton area rug from Summerhouse and distant mountain view. The owl sculpture is by Robert Adams.

ABOVE:
A remarkably peaceful and private property populated by hundreds of live oaks lies just minutes from downtown Sonoma. Designer Rossi Scott and her husband Angus bought it sight unseen and built a simple farmhouse based on Rossi's childhood memories of life in the borders of Scotland.

but unify it with the landscape. It's intimate and enclosed the way the trees surround you, with the landscape kind of holding you in."

The new home is a two-story, metal-roofed, gabled modern farmhouse clad in white board-and-batten. The living area comprises one space, open along its length to a deck partially covered by a cantilevered roof and framed by graceful oaks and deodar cedars. The lower level, housing a playroom and two bedrooms and unified by poured concrete floors, opens directly onto a concrete terrace. Dutch doors at both levels draw cool air from below on hot days (the house has no air-conditioning) and enhance the indoor-outdoor experience. Folding La Cantina doors in the living area and main bedroom open the house to the elements. Upstairs, ceramic wood floor tiles flow through all the rooms and out onto the deck for a seamless extension of the living space. Extra-tall windows inspired by European country homes come down low to the floor and are free of curtains or blinds. The effect is of a light-filled aerie.

The palette is minimal throughout, with white oak doors and woodwork and walls of plaster. In the daughter's room a blue and green scheme prevails; in the guest bedroom, green and white. A rec room features game tables, comfortable couches and a British-flag-draped ottoman. Unique touches include an all-white board-and-batten laundry and boot room with white oak cabinets and garage doors opening directly onto the gravel driveway. There Rossi accessorized with an array of antler mounts in the style of a Scottish hunting lodge. In the entry foyer, dressage saddles and fishing rods hung against oak walls constitute the only artwork. In the living room, the end wall housing the fireplace is painted a dark blue-green, matched on one wall in the master suite. In the bathrooms, where the floor tiles continue right into the sill-less showers, and guest bedroom there are accents of shiplap. All interior doors are unusually tall to enhance the sense of space.

Rossi worked hand-in-hand with David Sorenson and Ryan Eames of Eames Construction to design the interiors, exteriors and cabinetry for both buildings in a design-build process that unfolded organically. "Rossi's vision was already expressing itself when we first saw the property," says Eames. "The process was the epitome of teamwork; we were designing as we were buildings, and there's nothing your eyes land on that feels like it might have been the wrong decision."

Sorenson said that the homeowners brought a collaborative but uncompromising attitude. "Rossi was adamant about materials being authentic. She wanted the house to have the integrity of an old-world farmhouse, from indigenous Sonoma fieldstone to true board-and-batten siding to hand-troweled stucco to the lack of screens on doors and windows."

Explains Rossi, "For me, it represents a lot of memories of how I grew up and what I love in architecture, textiles and colors. My dream was that it would feel like a Scottish farmhouse standing gracefully on Sonoma Mountain."

PREVIOUS OVERLEAF:
David Sorenson and Ryan Eames of Eames Construction built to architect Nick Lee's structural specifications, while Rossi worked with the builders to design the interiors, exteriors and cabinetry for the house and barn. The white oak dining table and benches are from Archilinea; the caribou pelt hides are from Glacier Wear. Mindy Linkous's painting *Bridget Bardot* hangs over an antique cabinet from Summerhouse. The Kilim carpet is from Chelsea Antiques.

OPPOSITE:
The main bedroom opens fully to the outdoors with folding La Cantina door systems. The homeowner placed the vintage velvet Modena bed from RH against a wall painted a custom forest green from Color Folio Design. The reclaimed Russian oak night stand is from RH.

A light and airy boot room opens to the driveway for
ease of access with wet dogs and bags of groceries.
Eames Construction built the cedar cabinetry to Rossi's
specifications. The handles are from Rocky Mountain
Hardware. An existing water tank was clad in white cedar
and topped with a tin roof.

An array of roe antler mounts, sourced from Petworth Antiques in the UK, pay homage to the owners' upbringing in the English and Scottish countryside. The wall-mounted cross-handle faucet is from Waterworks, the vintage galvanized barn light from Cocoweb.

Rustic Estate

"Those of us who work in the wine country are very influenced by the hospitality experience."
— AMY A. ALPER

Set in Calistoga, at the northern end of the Napa Valley, this rustic estate rests on a bucolic site surrounded by rolling California hills. It also occupies a place—directly in the path of the region's 2017 wildfires—that is indelibly etched in the region's recent history. Although the blazes destroyed all of the neighboring homes and several adjacent outbuildings, this nearly completed home was spared, saved by the existing patios, rustic stone base and standing-seam metal roof that ground the project in the site and define its rural ambience.

For the clients—Calistoga winemakers, community volunteers and empty nesters—the project began as a renovation. Working with Sonoma-based architect Amy Alper, they quickly determined that the existing house would not allow them to live on the land in the way they envisioned. They would start over and design the house anew, but not from scratch. The new 4,250-square-foot home would be assembled within the site's original meandering walls, integrating numerous existing site features: an outdoor fireplace and kitchen, patios and pool, all of which would remain.

Carefully working the site plan around the existing site elements, Amy wove together old and new to create an ensemble of forms of varying heights and materials. The result is a house that feels as if it has evolved over time, which is typical of a rural property. From the entry pavilion, the first impression is a layered view across the great room, through the fourteen-foot pocketing doors, across the terrace and ending with the stately outdoor fireplace.

The materials help tell the story of the house, marrying a contemporary sensibility with a rustic palette. Inspired by the stone of the existing fireplace, the architect clad the home's three pavilion-like masses, which house the entry, kitchen and master bedroom, in native Napa Syar stone. To create a sense of development over time, she linked these three masses with walls of cedar in a board-and-batten pattern, and then drew the exterior materials inward to further define the interior spaces and create a textural connection between inside and out.

Layering is an integral part of the experience: the architecture is arranged to provide views through the spaces while the interior spaces, designed by Jennifer Robin, of Jennifer Robin Interiors, are a subtle ensemble of pattern and texture. Soft blues, hints of pattern in wallpaper and bathroom tile,

velvet pillows and soft carpets subtly counterbalance the building's more rustic finishes. The designer's consistent use of pure white—on walls, built-ins, sculptural light fixtures—is a particularly brilliant foil for the highly textured backdrop of stone and cedar.

"My goal with the interiors was to bring a sense of human scale and comfort to the spaces with texture and layering," says the designer. "I wanted to design with some drama, but the challenge was how to do this within a neutral palette and not detract from the surrounding landscape and views."

The great room is laid out in two zones: one to capture the view of Mt. St. Helena and the other focused on the television and interior space. Jennifer artfully linked the two zones with a double-sided chaise, using a mixture of antiques, varied textures and artwork to create a warm and welcoming space. A wall of white, customizable shelving highlights the owners' collection of art and artifacts.

Honoring the clients' request for a no-fuss kitchen, Amy chose to forego upper cabinets in favor of a wall of windows, designed a large island for gathering, and tucked an intimate built-in seating nook into the inviting space. Jennifer selected warm oak cabinets and reclaimed beams for their warmth and durable NuCrete counters as a hardworking alternative to marble counters (which were ruled out as impractical). She playfully alludes to those dreamed-of marble counters in the marble fabric covering the island pendants. Antique mirrored tile from Ann Sacks, used on backsplashes in both kitchen and dining room, reflects the views.

In what is perhaps the home's most impactful design element, Jennifer devised a horizontal pattern of soda-blasted oak paneling to cover freestanding walls in the dining room, master bedroom and guest room. The walls masterfully define the three spaces, drawing the outdoors in and adding a textured backdrop for other elements of the design. In the dining room, for example, a large table made of bleached reclaimed oak is surrounded by tan leather Roche Bobois chairs and is lit by a massive Avron white plaster pendant fixture from Bobo Interiors. This pendant is one of the designer's favorite pieces, and is a perfect complement to the oak wall that lies behind it.

This rustic retreat brings together the best parts of the wine country—old and new, modern and rustic, sophisticated but grounded in nature—and offers its owners a sanctuary from which they can witness the resilient wine country landscape recover and heal.

PREVIOUS OVERLEAF:
This house, designed by Amy A. Alper, Architect, with interiors by Jennifer Robin Interiors, weaves together old and new, rustic and sophisticated to tell an authentic story of living on the land.

OPPOSITE:
The materiality helps tell the story of the house, marrying a contemporary sensibility with rustic materials. Native Napa Syar, pulled into the interior, creates a bridge between the exterior and interior.

OPPOSITE:
In the kitchen, the architect chose to forego upper cabinets, instead ushering in the views. Oak cabinets and reclaimed beams are warm and inviting, while playful marble-print Rebecca Atwood fabric on the pendants alludes to wished-for marble counters replaced with more practical NuCrete.

ABOVE:
In the dining room, chairs by Roche Bobois pull up to a bleached oak dining table built by Statsky Design, topped by a massive white plaster Avron pendant fixture from Bobo Interiors, which pops against the horizontal soda-blasted oak covering the wall behind.

OPPOSITE:
A custom wall mural by Area Elements pays homage to the surrounding landscape, while hanging pendants from Urban Electric Company and bedside tables by Arteriors create an intimate sense of scale.

ABOVE:
One of the most distinctive elements of the interiors, a horizontal pattern of soda-blasted oak paneling covers free-standing walls in both the master bedroom and dining room. In the master bedroom, it provides a textural backdrop for the rattan bed; swing arm sconces by O'Lampia.

RIGHT:
A freestanding tub by Native Trails provides a perfect place to soak up the view.

RIGHT:
A view through the living room looks out onto the existing fireplace, outdoor kitchen and walls, which defined the site envelope for the new house. Artwork by James Lavadour—the client's own—lines the wall.

OVERLEAF:
A symmetrical view of the pool highlights the peacefulness of the bucolic site, characterized by rolling hills and the wine country's iconic oaks.

Nestled
in Nature

"On a beautiful day the door opens up and essentially becomes a pavilion; when the weather is inclement, you have all the attributes of a lovely enclosed interior."
— MICHAEL GUTHRIE

For Bay Area executives transitioning from a suburban environment, a vineyard property on a Sonoma mountainside proved the perfect setting for a year-round residence. Architect Michael Guthrie and contractor Jon Reiter of Reiter Fine Home Building worked in concert with the clients to design a vineyard retreat that took advantage of its hillside position 600 feet above the town of Sonoma to capture panoramic views and nearly endless sunlight.

Guthrie's H-shaped site plan created the opportunity for an entry court on the east side of the house and a family court arranged around the pool to the west, with both spaces defined by buildings, plantings and natural topography. The main residence is centered on the great room, with the owner's wing (bedroom suite, home gym and library) sited to the north. Three additional bedrooms and baths with a shared family room lie in a separate structure tethered to the main house by a covered breezeway. "The site plan was critical," says Guthrie, "and began to suggest what the floor plan should do. In this case, everything revolved around the great room, which enjoys a big panoramic glass door. On a beautiful day the door opens up and essentially becomes a pavilion. When the weather is inclement, you have all the attributes of a lovely enclosed interior."

Landscape architects Roche + Roche designed the entry experience, which begins at the bottom of the property with custom steel and wood gates flanked by stone walls and a meadow of creeping wild rye spotted with verbena and milkweed. The drive wends up between olive trees to a vineyard edged with a native plant garden that fosters beneficial insects, birds and reptiles. A bridge element of stacked stone with stone cobble guides visitors to the compound-like residence. The gravel parking area by the detached garage does double duty as a pétanque court.

The drama of the site is evident from the moment of arrival. The low central volume housing the public rooms is clad in stone and vertical stained cedar boards and topped with a standing-seam metal roof, yet it conveys a sense of transparency fostered by a wide span of sliding glass doors on both sides. These, whether open or closed, allow unimpeded views through the house and across Sonoma Valley to the mountains beyond.

Despite the promise inherent in the 1,000-bottle wine library in the foyer, the home is as much about the outdoors as the indoors, with full immersion

PREVIOUS OVERLEAF:
Architect Michael Guthrie
designed a home perched
600 feet above the town
of Sonoma as a full-time
residence for Bay Area
clients. Constructed by Reiter
Fine Home Building, the
exterior is defined by stone,
cedar and a standing-seam
metal roof, the interior by
walls of stone and plaster,
steel beams and sliding door
systems. Overlooking the
view on the west side, the
central volume opens out
onto a seating area with a
fireplace of board-formed
concrete, a dining area and
a pool with spa.

OPPOSITE:
In the kitchen, interior
designer Jeff Schlarb
installed neolith (virtually
indestructible, he says)
for the island's waterfall
countertop and marble tiles
for the backsplash. The Hicks
pendants are by Thomas
O'Brien for Visual Comfort.

OVERLEAF:
The open-plan living space,
which opens to the outdoors
on both sides, marries rustic
elements with exposed
structural steel. A custom
chandelier from John Pomp
hangs over Sloan Miyasato's
LUMA Collection Bog Oak
and Steel Strap table. Belle
Meade dining chairs are
covered in indoor-outdoor
fabric from Perennials.

in nature experienced from every room. The central great room—with a fireplace and seating area on one side, kitchen and pantry on the other, and dining table in the middle—is an architecturally dynamic space with Douglas fir trusses, steel tie rods and exposed steel beams and columns. A forty-five-foot span of glass opens to the covered outdoor living area, creating an uninterrupted extension of the living space. A dining area, a fireplace of board-formed concrete, and an infinity pool with spa draw visitors out to the edge of a meadow-like landscape, where the valley falls away below and one can just glimpse the northern tip of San Francisco Bay.

Inside and out, the atmosphere is one of architectural integrity and serenity. Designer Jeff Schlarb focused on the details of interior finishes and furnishings, from designing the fireplace to choosing stone and tile to refining the cabinetry profile. The clients, who are British, "embrace the California lifestyle, its casual quality and its indoor-outdoor aesthetic," explains Schlarb. "It's a beautiful estate but no one coming in would feel it was too regal." Natural materials were used whenever possible, in oak plank floors in the bedrooms, for instance, and marble in the master bath and kitchen backsplash, where it was cut into tiles for a modern look. Functionality guided certain choices, such as in the waterfall countertop in the kitchen, where Neolith was chosen for its near indestructibility. Schlarb employed the client's favorite autumn colors, burnt orange and warm whites, which paired well with the radiant-heat, colored-concrete floors, walnut casework and Venetian plaster. The overall effect, says the designer, "is a sophisticated version of rustic that feels and lives differently when you have all these elegant layers in a home."

Wine country living has at its heart a sustainable ethos that extends to the natural world. Roche + Roche installed owl boxes and bluebird houses to help control pests, and brought in custom wood and steel beehives to host native nesting bees which pollinate the garden and fruit orchard. They also designed multiple outdoor destinations on the property. These include a vegetable garden with raised steel beds, a custom water feature made from reclaimed steel augurs, and a firepit defined by a curved Cor-ten steel retaining wall, which is accessed by a gravel path that wends between native rock outcroppings. A one-mile loop of trails accesses hidden spots and varied views from the furthest outreaches of the property.

When Michael Guthrie was first contemplating the appropriate design and materiality for the project, he recalls, he would walk the site collecting twigs, rocks and other organic materials. These became inspiration for the home's palette, which relies on natural elements like re-sawn cedar that will weather over time and employs harmonious tones, such as those in the steel roof that reference the oak trees on the property's periphery. There's a reason the home is so well suited to site, he says. "It's all about paying attention to the natural surroundings."

The main bedroom suite opens to a private patio. A subdued palette—seen in the Jaipur rug, velvet-upholstered Brownstone Furniture bed and Vanguard benches with Brentano's custom Coloratura fabric—defers to the drama of the view.

A freestanding bathtub oriented toward a vine-covered
hillside creates a sublime sanctuary.

ABOVE:
From house to spa to pool to nature, the home fully
integrates into its mountainside site. The lounge chairs are
from Oasiq.

OPPOSITE:
Landscape designers Roche + Roche designed granite
paths that wend through the property to various outdoor
destinations, including a fruit orchard, a vegetable garden,
a custom water feature and a firepit area defined by a
curved Cor-ten steel retaining wall.

Refined Farmhouse

"This house is designed to be barefoot and jeans, topped with a silk shirt."
— PAULINA PERRAULT

Janet Hayes and her husband Jason Daniel searched for three years before finding the perfect parcel of land in the wine country. A native of Marin County, Janet has always loved the Napa Valley wine country, and the couple envisioned a weekend getaway for their family of four—a place where they could gather friends and family to enjoy the valley's slower pace of life. They wanted a flat parcel on the valley floor, with enough land to spread out, but not too much.

The site they found is perfectly situated between Calistoga and St. Helena, on a tree-lined lane that feels removed but is in fact close to every-thing. The couple, and their twin girls, fell in love with the lane, lined with iconic valley oaks. Not long before, their friends and neighbors the Hagans had purchased a similar parcel just down the street (that home is also included in this book), so when this second parcel became available they jumped on it. Describing the first time she walked the property, Janet says, "I couldn't breathe, it was so perfect. It was meant for us."

With a decades-long tenure as an executive in the home furnishings industry, Janet is a design leader, and she had a clear vision for their new home. She wanted a contemporary take on the farmhouse vernacular, executed primarily in black and white—a casual indoor-outdoor house with a refined aesthetic, designed to be lived in and enjoyed.

Janet turned to Marin County-based designer Paulina Perrault. Friends since their children were in kindergarten, Janet and Paulina each have strong design vision. They also share a large common denominator. Having known Janet for years, Paulina is able to discern and narrow the choices for her friend, and they are nearly always in line with Janet's vision. "We are amazingly in sync," says Paulina. "We're both fans of fiercely editing until the project becomes just what it needs to be." Casually elegant and effortlessly pulled together, Paulina describes the house as "barefoot and jeans, topped with a silk shirt."

Paulina introduced her clients to architects Jared Polsky, Rich Perlstein and Laura Van Amburgh at Polsky Perlstein Architects. The project started ambitiously, and then scaled down through the design process to be just what the clients needed, but no more. The couple had collected inspiration images showing tall, two-story structures with a strong sense of verticality and steep roof pitches. As it became clear that this house would be more

modest in scale, the challenge for the architects was to translate that sense of scale and verticality to a single-story structure.

"We spent a lot of time on the proportions, working to keep the gables narrow, lengthening the vertical windows and paying close attention to the pitch of the roof, not letting it get too low," says Laura. "As the scale was trimmed back, it became better and better."

At under 3,000 square feet with three bedrooms and two-and-a-half baths, this is not a large house, but its open plan, expansive covered porches, and multitude of places to gather both inside and out make it live far larger than its size. The U-shaped plan is straightforward, with kitchen and media room to one side and bedrooms to the other, linked by the open living and dining area defined by artfully milled passageways. The primary entry lies to the right of the symmetrical front facade, but expansive doorways on both front and back facades can be thrown open to create a contiguous indoor-outdoor space that flows easily and accommodates gatherings large and small. The rear facade faces south toward the vineyards, creating the illusion of a far larger site.

"The whole valley is their backyard," says Rich.

Sheltered outdoor space is key to living in this part of the wine country, where the temperatures can soar in the summer and early fall. Outdoor dining, kitchen and entertaining spaces align under trellises and roofed areas for an atmosphere that is low key. The outdoor entertaining kitchen, complete with outdoor television for sporting events, was Jason's dream. "It's the only part of the house I let him have on his own," jokes Janet. "The rest of it was mine."

Janet was looking for a very specific take on the farmhouse aesthetic, eschewing many of its trappings to create an effect that is highly sophisticated. The vision moved in an increasingly contemporary direction as the design progressed: millwork was simplified, fixtures and fitting choices became more streamlined.

A self-professed "millwork girl," Paulina's passion lies in the details of the interior architecture. Years of experience working directly with developers and builders fueled her passion, leading to a practice in which she works closely with architects on every detail of the interior. "The architecture team was so generous," says the designer. "They let me run with it." This house was, in fact, a truly collaborative effort, with the architecture team, interior designer and clients all actively working through each decision.

Paulina's favorite memory revolves around the porch swing, which had been on the couple's wish list from the beginning. When custom options proved to be inordinately costly, Jason found another more affordable option, a swing crafted in Pennsylvania by the Amish. The swing illustrates the project in miniature: design-driven, collaborative, resourceful and, in the end, just right.

PREVIOUS OVERLEAF:
The result of a true collaboration between the owners, architects Polsky Perlstein and interior designer Paulina Perrault, this home is casual but sophisticated. Landscape architects Lucas and Lucas created an overall vision for the property and planting; then architects, designer and clients all made contributions to the final design.

OPPOSITE:
The dining room table is really the daily table—this is wine country, and the atmosphere is casual.

OVERLEAF:
Executed primarily in black and white, this is a casual indoor-outdoor house with a refined aesthetic, designed to be lived in and enjoyed. Sofas, pillows and area rugs by Williams Sonoma Home. Artwork over the mantel was selected by the owner.

BELOW:
Paulina tucked an AV closet, broom closet and Hestan
wine refrigerator into the laundry room, adjacent to the
kitchen. Farmhouse sink by Franke and pendant light by
Williams Sonoma Home.

RIGHT:
The design is a very specific take on the farmhouse
vernacular, eschewing many of its trappings to create
an effect that is highly sophisticated. Backsplash tile by
Jeffrey Court, pendant lights by Visual Comfort, counter
stools by Williams Sonoma Home, kitchen appliances
by Hestan, in the company's first residential installation.

ABOVE:
Nearly everyone challenged owner Janet Hayes on the size
of the pool, but it had always been part of her vision. When
asked why she wanted such a large pool, her answer was,
"Why wouldn't I?"

OPPOSITE ABOVE:
Life here is lived indoors and outdoors in equal measure.
Outdoor furnishings by Williams Sonoma Home.

OPPOSITE BELOW:
Together the design team decided to relocate six mature
olive trees that existed on the site to create an allée leading
to the rain man sculpture they reclaimed from the site's
previous home.

A Cottage Reborn

"The project really was a series of interventions into a traditional house."
— GREG MOTTOLA

Set on a modest one-acre parcel on the floor of the Napa Valley, Tom and Laurie Poggi's weekend home is an island within a sea of vineyards. Though the 360-degree view now defines their wine country experience, the original home was remarkably closed off from the site and vineyards.

Long-time residents of San Francisco, the couple had purchased the farmhouse in 2004, and then lived in it for over a decade. Both work in industries driven by long-term relationships (he in commercial real estate, she in private equity), so when they decided to renovate, it was only natural they turn to Greg Mottola, principal at Bohlin Cywinski Jackson, and his team. Tom and Laurie had each worked with Greg on commercial projects over the years and trusted him implicitly.

Tom and Laurie produce Cabernet Sauvignon under their brand Poggi Wines. Their initial goal was to adapt the garage to add a crush pad for wine-making, a plan that proved infeasible due to zoning. However, after Greg invited the couple to visit one of the firm's more contemporary residential projects just a few hours away in Sacramento, the project quickly pivoted, gaining steam as the team explored ways to open up the couple's farmhouse and connect it to the landscape. "I guess you might say wine-making was the initial focus and visiting the Sacramento house was the catalyst," says Laurie. The resulting design is a distinct blend of farmhouse and contemporary, carried out in a way that leaves the ethos of each idiom distinct.

The team knew it was important to maintain the traditional farmhouse character from the street, while opening the house up in the back in a more contemporary arrangement of indoor-outdoor spaces. While the size of the home's footprint remains roughly the same, an expanded wraparound porch on three sides opens the house up in a way that allows it to feel much larger than its actual footprint. The elevated porch lifts the views up and over the surrounding vineyards. The new kitchen and dining area, redesigned around an expansive central island, now opens directly to the broad expanse of porch through sliding doors that pocket away into the walls, allowing an effortless indoor-outdoor flow.

Amid a series of ideas, one decision set the tone for the rest of the project. By respacing the front porch columns, the team moved the front door to the center of the front facade, shifting it away from the internal stair and aligning it with the walkway that bisects the twin palms marking the

entry to the property. Suddenly, what had once been an awkward transition became an organizing principle. "Once we made the decision to move the front door, everything else just started falling into place," says Shawn Wood, project architect. "That front door changed everything," Laurie agrees.

One of the most significant design moves occurred upstairs, where the team deconstructed the existing rooms to create a fully integrated master bedroom and bath. What had been a series of dark, nearly viewless rooms tucked up under the eaves is now an open loft, flooded with light from two new skylights. The master suite fully inhabits the roof form; the folds of the all-white walls follow the existing roofline in a complex work of origami. With no door to the master suite, the stair becomes the transitional element. Rendered in a semitransparent pattern of vertical cedar slats, the stairway is a sculptural element in itself.

Tasked with the design of both the architecture and the interiors, the team at Bohlin Cywinski Jackson kept it simple. The interiors are a calming blend of wood, white and gray basalt. Within the limited color palette, varied textures create visual interest. "We ditched all the furniture," says Tom enthusiastically. "We trusted BCJ with the design and the feeling is incredibly cohesive."

Landscape designers EinwillerKuehl transformed the gardens, inverting the landscape and hardscape to create an entirely different experience of the site. Stone that once surrounded the existing pool was replaced with grass, making the pool area all the more inviting in the hot climate of the northern Napa Valley. Grasses soften the transition between the garden and adjacent vineyards, and an outdoor shower built of ipe hardwood fulfills a long-held wish.

Rendered in an approachable scale, this home is eminently livable, and its universal appeal is striking. Tom and Laurie love sitting on the front porch and listening to passersby exclaim, "Oh, that is my dream house." (This happens often.)

Above all, this newly reborn farmhouse brings its owners a palpable sense of joy. Asked to describe their home, words come easily. Tom effortlessly recites adjectives—"clean, simple, uncluttered, practical, warm, welcoming." Laurie quickly adds, "It's just enough."

LEFT:
The wood interiors are warm and inviting. "People come to visit and they just don't want to leave," asserts owner Laurie Poggi. Custom cabinets constructed by Fairweather Associates are clad in vertical-grain hemlock.

ABOVE:
Though the house is on the valley floor, it is elevated just enough to have sweeping views. "It changes everything," says owner Tom Poggi.

ABOVE:
Texture and detail stand out. Homeowner Laurie Poggi couldn't explain why she loved running her hand along the bamboo railing on her way up or down the stairs until the architect explained it was designed just slightly smaller than the norm, making it fit more easily into the clasp of her hand.

RIGHT:
A limited palette of materials is used in a variety of finishes and textures. For example, basalt stone is installed in polished, honed and rough applications, illustrated on the living room fireplace.

BELOW:
With no door to the master suite, the stair forms a transitional element, the vertical cedar slats becoming a sculptural element in themselves.

RIGHT:
Upstairs, a fully integrated master suite is tucked up under the eaves, the folds of the all-white walls following the existing roofline in a complex work of origami. Floors are whitewashed reclaimed Douglas fir, and custom cabinets are vertical-grain Hemlock.

OVERLEAF:
It was important to maintain the traditional farmhouse character from the street, opening the house up in the back in a more contemporary arrangement of indoor-outdoor spaces.

Historic Meets Modern

"We wanted to preserve the street presentation so that people who walk by wouldn't see that anything had changed." — LUKE WADE

For almost two decades, Keith and Cherie Hughes lived on a twenty-three-acre organic vineyard amidst twelve acres of grapes. There they became deeply attuned to patterns of weather and season, and were fully enmeshed in the day-to-day operations of producing Chardonnay, Syrah and Zinfandel wines under the Hughes Family Vineyards label.

Country life held myriad pleasures, but over time they found themselves drawn to the attractions of town. A circa 1909 Craftsman bungalow near the heart of downtown Sonoma proved too interesting an opportunity to resist—and not just because the local landmark had made an appearance in the 1973 hit *American Graffiti*. Its charming facade, its mature trees and bucolic creek, its setback from the street, and most of all, its long narrow lot offered the opportunity to experience the best of both worlds: in-town living and the utmost in privacy, historic authenticity and a dramatic contemporary addition. With the creative talent of Wade Design Architects, Earthtone Construction, Jennifer Robin Interiors and Rozanski Design landscape designers, it would also manifest the best of the indoor-outdoor lifestyle that makes the wine country so appealing.

The path to construction was circuitous due to the home's placement within Sonoma's historic overlay district. After the Hughes hired a local historic architect, commissioned a historical report and slowly worked their way through the design review process, the project was ultimately approved, along with instructions to preserve the original structure as authentically as possible while designing any addition in a significantly different style and tone. "The city felt that anything new should be of its own era," Cherie said.

For first-time visitors to the house, this results in a surprising reveal. The traditional porch, with its custom-made hanging swing, and the intimate parlor, with its cozy seating and restored fireplace, are very much 1909, albeit refreshed in a more contemporary sensibility. That approach is carried out as well in the upstairs study and two guest suites tucked under the dormered eaves. Beyond the parlor, though, the true nature of the project unveils itself. First, a dramatic vaulted living room with adjacent kitchen is flanked by built-in banquette seating against a white stone-clad wall. This leads to the dining area, which provides a glassy connector to a more contemporary building housing the owners' suite at ground level and an upstairs office, guest room and gym.

PREVIOUS OVERLEAF:
When the owners of Hughes
Family Vineyards discovered
a pristine 1909 Craftsman
bungalow on a large lot in
downtown Sonoma, they
made the move from country
to city. Wade Design Architects
and Earthtone Construction
reinvigorated the historic home
with grace and authenticity,
added a contemporary addition
and rebuilt an old barn. Two
roomy swings visible from
the street provide the perfect
perches for waving to the
neighbors. The leaded glass
windows are original to the
house.

RIGHT:
The team agreed that the
home's original parlor should
be left with its vintage charm
intact. With an adjustable-
height table by Matthew Chase
Woodwork and Sabin Ojai Tub
chairs in Holly Hunt outdoor
fabric, the room is the perfect
place to spend a quiet evening.
The horn and chrome lamps
are from Louise Bradley; the
rug is Chista. The Corbin Bronze
sculptures add a touch of
whimsy.

The contrast between old and new only serves to heighten the drama, explains architect Luke Wade. The low-ceilinged dining space has clean lines, white walls, contemporary lighting and floor-to-ceiling windows that slide and pocket between back-to-back fireplaces. It opens out to a full outdoor living area with a dining table, a lounge centered on the concrete fireplace, and a full kitchen and island with counter seating. With the barriers removed to the outdoors, the step down to the landscaped garden and the pool with its cascading water feature becomes an integral part of the experience of the home. "There was a nice simplicity to the early Craftsman home," Wade says. "We wanted to preserve the street presentation so that people who walk by wouldn't see that anything had changed, while making it a surprise journey for those who enter."

Jennifer Macdonald, founder of Jennifer Robin Interiors, was tasked with integrating the history of the home and the owners' aesthetic. "The design challenge on this project was creating a perfect balance," she explains. "We needed to honor the historic relevance of the home yet provide the modern and crisp look the clients desired. The interiors needed to stay quiet to highlight the clients' art collection, the architecture and the landscape. We focused on layering texture and interest that is slowly discovered and appreciated the longer one spends time in the home."

Any in-town project presents unique challenges and considerations. The team from Earthtone Construction had to maneuver within very tight physical constraints and around existing trees, a significant task on a job requiring a lot of large equipment. And working with existing structures adds a layer of complexity, says Andy Bannister. "It's never easy working with homes of this age that are often not up to current code and have been remodeled in the past. You can often conceal imperfections while still bringing a house up to current code, but a modern feel as this one has is a lot less forgiving."

Ultimately, the home offers so many ways of living, from its public front porch to its private garden, from its expansive open spaces suitable for large events to its intimate spaces for two in the historic sitting room.

But the project was very much about recreating the benefits of country living in the heart of town, says Luke Wade. "The clients were relocating from a beautiful, well-landscaped vineyard estate property to a neighborhood. We wanted to recreate the garden setting and privacy." To that end, all interior spaces open out to courtyards, while property lines are screened with lush plantings. The main courtyard focuses on the pool and fountain, while the spa sits in a private space off the master suite. The result, says Wade, is "a shaded oasis in the middle of an historic neighborhood."

Within the new construction in the heart of the home, the sitting area is neutral and textured. The Kroll sofa is upholstered in Chivasso fabric; the Conique Chandelier is by Mattaliano.

ABOVE:
The fireplace is set within a stone-clad wall and flanked by built-in benches in a room that has its own character despite being open to the dining area and the outdoors. Anees swivel armchairs are upholstered in Liaigre leather, while a television hides behind a commissioned artwork by Brigitte McReynolds.

OPPOSITE ABOVE:
The dining area serves as transition from the old to the new part of the home. Interior designer Jennifer Macdonald of Jennifer Robin Interiors worked closely with the owners to create crisp, contemporary interiors while honoring the history of the home. The Jonathan Browning Chamont Chandelier is suspended over a custom dining table from Gabe Statsky.

OVERLEAF:
Fully retractable glass walls from Jada open the home to the outdoors for effortless entertaining and constant immersion in nature. The dining chairs by Bright Chair Company, upholstered in Holly Hunt leather, are light yet comfortable. *Always Asking*, a wire wall sculpture by Pamela Dernham, hangs over the fireplace.

PAGES 109–109:
Paul Rozanski and his team at Rozanski Design created the plan for the football-field-shaped lot, which has the street on one side and a creek and woods at its far end. The landscape and pool design makes full use of the property and conjures a world removed from the bustle of town. The pool with water feature, outdoor kitchen, fireplace and living area, and terrace stepping directly from the living room gives the owners the feel of a private spa. The outdoor furnishings are by Janus et Cie.

The Bird House

"I wanted this to be the quintessential Jacobsen house." — JEFF ATLAS

Jeff Atlas first met architect Hugh Newell Jacobsen over two decades ago. He recalls confiding to the famed architect, "I'm really a frustrated architect," to which Hugh replied with a wry smile, "Me too."

Not many clients are as well-versed in architecture as Jeff Atlas. Raised in Washington DC, where Hugh Newell Jacobsen established his eponymous office in 1958, Jeff had an obsession with architecture from an early age—and an admiration for this architect in particular. From their first meeting, the two men felt an immediate kinship. The architect's wife would later comment that she had never heard Hugh have such a deep conversation about architecture with anyone but another architect.

Jeff later moved to San Francisco, lived on the city's famous Lombard Street and built a successful career in advertising. "Architecture and advertising are similar," he declares. "Ideally, both are arts that have to be functional." When he finally purchased a beautiful hilltop parcel with sweeping views of the Napa Valley, he turned to his favorite architect—and Hugh's son Simon, who had since joined the practice—to design his dream house.

The subject of numerous books, the recipient of six National Honor Awards from the American Institute of Architects and a member of the Architectural Digest Hall of Fame, Hugh Newell Jacobsen is well known for his pared-down aesthetic and his distinctive interpretation of the American vernacular—simple gabled forms (often white), a limited palette of materials and details whittled down to the essentials. Jeff envisioned a small house with all of the architect's signature elements. "I wanted this to be the quintessential Jacobsen house," says Jeff. "Every element he is known for is deliberately included in this home."

This is Jeff's weekend home. At just 1,850 square feet—comprising a great room with kitchen, two bedrooms, two baths and a small office—it is a condensed version of the architect's greatest hits. The scale of the house enforces a certain discipline and restraint that pairs perfectly with the architect's approach. Designed to be timeless, everything is symmetrical, and every detail is fully considered. Nearly anything that can be hidden is tucked away: rain flows into slotted drains to accommodate a gutterless roofline, interior air vents and shades are hidden in soffits, kitchen cabinets are streamlined with no visible hardware. Even the large sliding exterior doors are free of hardware.

Every experience in the journey through this house is carefully calibrated, beginning with the arrival. A private drive curves up the hill through an allée of olive trees, culminating in a circular gravel parking area. The first view of the house is iconic: a repeated composition of the simple forms for which the architect is known. "It's kind of like jazz," Jeff remarks. "It's all about theme and variation." Carried out in a crisp white set against the cerulean Napa sky and topped with a standing-seam metal roof in a very proper nod to the agrarian vernacular, this is farmhouse style expressed with the utmost decorum.

Inside, serenity reigns. Every surface is rendered in Hugh's signature shade of white, and adornment is kept to a minimum. Lofty, gabled ceilings in the three primary living spaces heighten the sense of space, and in the great room a series of small dormers floods the interior with light. The rear facade is entirely given over to the view, with a wall of glass punctuated by simple white mullions creating frames that render the vineyards below an otherworldly shade of green. The rear terrace is designed for entertaining, which Jeff does often. Connected to the kitchen by a pass-through window, the outdoor dining area is shaded by a simple trellis. The terrace's travertine was selected specifically because it resists absorbing the heat of the afternoon sun. Blue tiles line the infinity pool, allowing the edge to disappear into the valley view.

PREVIOUS OVERLEAF:
Set overlooking the vineyards on an idyllic Napa Valley site, The Bird House—designed by iconic East Coast architect Hugh Newell Jacobsen and his son Simon—is one man's homage to his favorite architect.

OPPOSITE:
The first view of the house is iconic, a repeated composition of the simple forms for which the architect is well known.

ABOVE:
The pared-back interiors allow the structure of the architecture and the sweeping views of the Napa Valley below to take center stage. Furnishings are vintage Knoll originals, sourced by owner Jeff Atlas.

Not surprisingly, Jeff—who selected the furnishings himself—started by asking himself what Hugh would do. Nearly all of the interior furnishings are vintage Knoll originals, accumulated while the house was under construction. Jeff was meticulous about his sourcing. Some of the furnishings, such as simply constructed bedside tables of stainless steel, marble and Lucite, he built himself on weekends. Prints by Frank Stella, Josef Albers, Wayne Thiebaud and Gene Davis line the walls, and books about art and design fill the iconic Jacobsen "egg crate" bookshelves. And, of course, there are the birdhouses—gifts from friends to celebrate the completion of his home.

Quoting from one of his favorite movies, the 1948 film *Mr. Blandings Builds his Dream House*, Jeff confides: "There are some things you should buy with your heart and not with your head."

ABOVE:
All-white interiors evoke a
distinct sense of serenity,
allowing the views to provide
the drama.

RIGHT:
Multiple dormers, set within
a steeply pitched standing-
seam metal roof, are one of the
architect's trademark design
elements.

ABOVE:
The owner, who selected the furnishings himself, started by asking himself what Hugh would do, filling the house with vintage Knoll originals, and a few pieces he built himself on the weekends.

OVERLEAF:
Owner Jeff Atlas likens the architecture of his beloved home to jazz: "It's all about theme and variation."

Wine Country
Contemporary

Black Box House

"What is special about this project is that everyone is able to have a distinct experience, taking away a piece of the overall experience for themselves." — GEORGE BEVAN

Originally from Chicago, the owners of this striking home behind the town of Sonoma had fallen in love with the picturesque town and with the Sonoma County wine country. They acquired their twenty-four-acre hillside site, filled with oaks, manzanitas and stone outcroppings, from the Sonoma Land Trust with a conservation easement. The land was familiar territory for George Bevan, principal of Bevan & Associates, who has been designing homes in the Northern California wine country for years.

Wishing to preserve the landscape, George and his clients opted to leave the site as untouched as possible, immersing the project into it with a minimum of clearing. "Matching what the site dictates and what the human inhabitants want is always an interesting process," says the architect.

Fitting the house into the landscape, rather than making the landscape accommodate the house, entailed a rigorous exercise in site planning. George worked with Mike Lucas of Lucas & Lucas Landscape Architecture—a frequent collaborator and longtime friend—who helped him preserve existing landscape and tuck the house and hardscape into the site. The result is a series of black boxes that tumble down the hillside. In essence, George developed an archetype and repeated it, deconstructing the program and scattering its pieces and parts throughout the landscape. Linked by gravel pathways, the house totals nearly 6,000 square feet, but the deconstructed design and dark hue mask its scale as it settles into its surroundings.

In the main house, the living area takes center stage, flanked by the kitchen on one side and master suite on the other. Above the master suite, his-and-her offices with views of the treetops are linked by a covered terrace. A separate garage forms a gallery-like space for the husband's cherished collection of cars. Inspired by the hospitality experience, George stepped the three guest cottages down the hillside, connected by a covered walkway. In an approach prescient to an era where social distancing may become part of our new normal, each cottage opens to the pool and pool house, and guests retain their own unique experience of the site.

George Bevan doesn't usually give it all away at once, preferring to layer the experiences of the site and visual field so he can unveil them in sequence. However, with this project he took a different tack, putting the view on full display with a transparent entry that provides a sight line clear through the house to the wall of windows and the vista beyond. The green

PREVIOUS OVERLEAF:
George Bevan, principal of
Bevan + Associates, designed
this house to provide a unique
indoor-outdoor experience of the
wooded site, as well as a gallery
for the husband's cherished
collection of cars, including this
vintage Range Rover.

LEFT:
The architect put the view on full
display with a transparent entry
that provides views clear through
the house to the wall of windows
and the vista beyond. The custom
exterior shou sugi ban siding is
by Delta Millworks, windows and
doors are by Fleetwood Windows
& Doors, and the entry light
fixture is by Bega.

The architect's touch is
evident in the kitchen, with
sleek custom cabinetry
clad in oak, a monumental
island sheathed in steel
and a large sliding window
from Fleetwood Windows &
Doors. Custom cabinetry is
by Johannes Van Moorick,
custom steel island is by
Schnitzkraft, appliances are
by Gaggenau, and fixtures
are by Dornbracht.

ABOVE:
The kitchen, dining area
and terrace seamlessly
integrate indoor and outdoor
experiences. Table and chairs
are by Pininfarina, rug is from
Tufenkian, and pendant light
is by Gabriel Scott.

and gold of the hillside in the near view and the valley in the distance are visible at every turn, becoming the home's primary artwork. Adjacent to the entry, kitchen windows pocket into the wall to usher the outside in. From the exterior the punched opening forms yet another dramatic frame for the panorama.

Inside, the interiors are spare and almost meditative. Everything is tucked away, and decor is kept to a minimum. The owners selected the furnishing and finishes, with help from George. The architect's signature is visible in the kitchen, where clean-lined cabinets and a hefty island sheathed in steel are a glamorous touch within the relatively restrained interior palette. In another room, cabinets of hot-rolled steel form a pattern that echoes the surrounding hills.

When asked why he chose to cloak the house in black, George explains that nature is often dense, and in the shadows—the spaces between—it is dark. If he wanted to fit the house into the "spaces between," a dark hue simply made sense. The shou sugi ban cladding—a burned-wood finish native to Japan—is also naturally resistant to fire, a very real danger in the hills of the wine country. When queried on his choice of an all-white interior, his answer is simple. "It's still a house," he smiles, "I wanted it to feel clean and refreshing." The contrast provides a distinct sense of drama and highlights the ever-changing play of light on this hillside site.

ABOVE:
The living room is all about the view. The sofa is by Roche Bobois, the cocktail is by Timothy Oulton, the rug by Tufenkian and the light fixture by RH.

OPPOSITE:
Hot-rolled steel takes on a pattern reminiscent of the neighboring mountain ranges.

OVERLEAF:
Guest cottages enjoy their own unique connections to the outdoors and pool. Outdoor Magis Spun Chairs are from Design Within Reach, linens are by Brooklinen and pillows are from RH.

LEFT:
"When you look at nature, especially when it is dense, there is a lot of darkness and shadow in the spaces between," says the architect. Placing the house in the "spaces between," and choosing a dark color for the exterior, was a natural choice.

ABOVE:
The restrained palette of materials makes a strong statement in the wooded setting, particular when contrasted against a cerulean sky. Outdoor furnishings from RH.

Vintner's View

"We imagined kids running in and out (we even sampled concrete wet to see if it was slippery), with everyone having meals together." — ELIOT SUTRO

For a San Francisco family living in a traditional Edwardian during the week, their wine country weekend retreat would be the opposite in style: contemporary, compact, understated, muted in palette, anchored into the landscape and filled with light. It would also be eco-conscious and energy efficient, a factor that drove all the choices for materials and furnishings. The result is a home at one with its place amidst the vines on a hilltop overlooking Healdsburg's Dry Creek Valley.

The project kicked off with the same architect and interior designer who had collaborated on the extensive remodel of the family's Edwardian. Sutro Architects and Adeeni Design Group were able to hit the ground running from the first visit to the property, during which they walked the eighteen-acre site to discuss the most fortuitous placement and orientation of the home. Arterra Landscape Architects and Upscale Construction joined the team, helping weigh the options for a new house on the hillside that would enjoy views without being visible from below, and the original structure, a small abode nestled in the trees (so small, in fact, that during the year the owners stayed there, the kids slept in bunk beds in the garage).

The owners envisioned a house within a vineyard; at the same time, they wanted to disturb the landscape as little as possible. Entirely surrounded by Cabernet Sauvignon, Cabernet Franc and Merlot vines, the two-level home is built into the hillside, with concrete retaining walls following the contours of the landscape. The scale is modest and low impact. The public rooms open fully to the outdoors while the owners' private suite is a tranquil retreat. The big open room downstairs was designed by the three kids; their space has multiple bunk bed configurations and its own basketball patio. On its west side, smaller windows and three maples (which also provide fall color and a place to string a hammock) help manage the intense sun.

"The house was built using passive house ideology," explains Stephen Sutro. "It's super insulated and oriented so that the sun doesn't penetrate and generate too much heat during hot summer days. Expansive windows facing north toward the primary views allow a lot of glass without a lot of sun. This house has no air conditioning, but it doesn't get too hot because the mass of concrete keeps the temperature stable."

The unique experience of the home is announced upon arrival, as it has no formal driveway. Guests park near the original structure and then ascend

a Cor-ten steel stairway to a path of decomposed granite lined with lavender that leads up through the vineyard, past concrete retaining walls and raised Cor-ten steel beds planted in vegetables, to a level expanse comprising the pool area. With an outdoor shower and kitchen, hot tub, and contemporary steel and wood arbor with raised concrete firepit, the outdoor space fully engages with the upper level of the home, whose roof extends toward the pool to create an ample covered patio. "The pool is a central part of the experience," explains Eliot Sutro. "We imagined kids running in and out (we even sampled concrete wet to see if it was slippery), with everyone having meals together. Our clients were not interested in an overscaled house."

In both architecture and furnishings, there was disciplined focus on using fewer materials. The simplified palette is expressed in reclaimed barnwood siding; concrete floors, fireplaces, countertops, and backsplash; cedar ceilings; and large expanses of glass. Walnut was chosen for cabinetry, stairs, furniture and bathroom sconces, teak for dining chairs and outdoor furniture, steel for the hood and countertop, and bronze for hardware.

The interiors were kept simple and casual, furthering the goals of livability. Fabrics are comfortable and subdued, while the furnishings are a mix of new, custom and vintage. An outdoor end table was handcrafted from a tree from the wife's father's property. The three interchangeable dining tables (made from reclaimed barnwood, to speak to the siding) are on wheels so they can be used inside or out in various configurations. Over-counter shelves are open for ease of access, while a large kitchen window acts as a pass-through to the dining table by the pool. The application of cedar and walnut on the ceiling and in the kitchen cabinetry warms up the open living spaces, defined by white walls, concrete floors, walls of glass, and a board-formed concrete fireplace. Mouth-blown custom kitchen pendants based on a 1970s design speak to the clients' interest in mid-century style, while a grape-like cluster chandelier adds a sense of airiness without impeding the view.

For much of the year, explains designer Claudia Juestel, "Healdsburg is hot and sunny, so the goal was a light and airy space with a fresh white backdrop. (We tried six samples of white wall color because there was so much green coming in from the vineyard and hills.) We agreed to put color very strategically into the art and accessories to keep with the calm vibe they were going for, and we limited the palette to the colors of the vineyard." These pops of green appear in the kitchen counter stools, the built-in fireplace bench, the powder room mirror, and a vintage cast-iron sink. Juestel worked with local artists on custom designs, including a weaver who hand-wove fabric with light green stripes from organic linen yarns and alpaca for the throw pillows.

The overall effect is not only cohesive, says Eliot Sutro, but "a warm version of contemporary. That is intentional and speaks to the character of the family."

ABOVE:
Pops of lime green appear
throughout the house. The
cast-iron sink is vintage.

RIGHT:
Open shelving and a waterfall
countertop treatment create
clean lines, while a pass-
through from the kitchen to
the patio makes for effortless
entertaining. In the spirit of
using fewer materials, Juestel
chose the same concrete
for all countertops and the
backsplash. To avoid the grout
lines that come with tile, she
had a single sheet of concrete
embossed with a texture for
interest. The silver mirror
induction cooktop blends
in with the stainless-steel
countertop surrounding it. The
clients like midcentury design
and chose custom mouth-
blown pendants in the kitchen
based on a 1970s design in
metal.

PREVIOUS OVERLEAF:
The chandelier over the dining table is suspended slightly
higher than usual in order to avoid blocking the view; the
choice of an airy fixture with grape-like glass balls furthers
that goal. Juestel worked with a local artist to hand-weave
the fabric for the throw pillows from organic linen yarns
and colored alpaca. The end table was made from a tree
trunk from the wife's father's property.

ABOVE:
The furniture in the dining area and on the terrace is
interchangeable. The tables are made from reclaimed barn
wood, echoing the siding, and are mounted on wheels to
create different combinations. The chairs are teak and the
views are endless.

Winged Retreat

"It is a remarkable site, with views of one layer of ridgeline after another."
— JOSHUA AIDLIN

Architects Joshua Aidlin and David Darling have made a continual effort in their years of practice to develop architecture that engages each of the senses. This goal—a sort of "true north" for their eponymous firm—has resulted in a remarkable tradition. The two partners begin every project by camping together on the site, absorbing all of its sensory input and forming a visceral connection to the land.

After camping on the site for this home in the Santa Lucia Preserve, a community in Carmel Valley dedicated to preserving natural resources and living in harmony with nature, the partners were struck by the plethora of angles in the surrounding ridgelines. "It is a remarkable site, with views of one layer of ridgeline after another," recalls Joshua.

Their clients were two retiring doctors who chose to move out of the city and embrace nature. In order to design a home that would coexist with the site without dominating it, the architects needed to follow the ridgelines. Thus the vision for the Winged Retreat emerged, born from the concept of a bird alighting on the site, adding to the natural surroundings without fundamentally changing their composition.

The resulting home is composed of volumes that follow the slope of the hill, with the uphill volume containing a garage and a second-story deck, and the lower volumes housing the main living spaces. Inside, open spaces minimize circulation, helping to keep the home's footprint small. Half of the house burrows into the hillside while the other reaches dramatically out toward the west with the hillside falling away below. The three shed roofs are a nod to the agricultural language of the Carmel Valley, and in their cantilevered form they look remarkably like wings.

Nestled amidst groves of oak and madrone trees that offer shade and screen it from neighbors and the road, the structure all but disappears into the landscape. An abundance of glass and natural materials such as cedar siding, walnut flooring, and ipe decks connect the structure to the landscape. The wing-like rooflines extend into deep eaves, which reach out over the expansive decks and shade the interiors. The sculptured undersides of the eaves act as a light ballast, throwing light deep into the interiors, while the clerestory windows usher in the low rays of the winter sun and diffuse daylight year-round.

The atmosphere within is hushed, with a distinct sense of calm. The purposefully quiet entry facade yields to an interior oriented to embrace the natural surroundings. The westerly facades, composed primarily of glass, frame dramatic views of the ridgelines. The level ceiling in the main spaces pitches upward toward clerestory windows on the south facade to frame the views of the uphill trees. Visible through the living room's windows is evidence of the building's harmony with the site: the angle of the roofline is in perfect alignment with the ridgeline.

Joshua attributes the house's noticeable hush to its "concert-level acoustics." The ceiling in the living room is covered with a stretched fabric and ducts are covered to baffle extraneous sound and allow their clients to enjoy both the sounds of nature, and music, unimpeded.

The couple longed for a quiet refuge, but they also wanted a place where they could entertain guests. The center of the home is arranged for entertaining—a constellation of kitchen, indoor and outdoor dining, cantilevered deck, outdoor fireplace and hot tub. The C-shaped house wraps around the outdoor dining area, protecting it from the prevailing winds, while a twenty-foot long screen drops down from the trellis above to shield the dining area from insects, which in this heavily wooded area can be ferocious.

The private areas of the home are intimate and lovingly detailed. In the master bedroom, a custom-designed bed built of slatted walnut panels is backlit to provide textured lighting. Operable fins on the guest bedroom window are automated, providing complete privacy when closed and turning the small room into a lantern overlooking the pool when opened at night. Joshua added small studies to the adjacent his and her walk-in closets that, though completely separate, look out to the same view and connect via a small peek-a-boo window. In the master bath the cabinetry was custom designed for the wife's physique, allowing her to comfortably age in place—the type of thoughtful design solution that makes this house fit its occupants like a tailored suit of clothing.

Hand-crafted and seamlessly connected to the site in gestures both large and small, this house is a testament to the value of spending a few nights on the land.

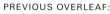

PREVIOUS OVERLEAF:
Architect Joshua Aidlin designed this home for a retiring couple who chose to leave the city and embrace nature. Inspired by the concept of a bird alighting on the site, the home's wing-like rooflines extend into deep eaves, which reach out over the expansive decks.

ABOVE:
The level ceiling in the main spaces pitches upward toward clerestory windows on the south facade. The angle of the roofline, in perfect alignment with the ridgeline, is evidence of the structure's harmony with the site.

OVERLEAF:
Crafted of a limited palette of walnut and stainless steel, the kitchen speaks to the surroundings and echoes the uncluttered essence of the design. A back-painted glass back-splash lifts up to reveal small appliances; white waterfall countertops serenely top the island, and custom lighting was a collaboration with Boyd Lighting.

OPPOSITE:
In the master bedroom, a
custom bed of slatted walnut
panels, designed by Aidlin
Darling Design and fabricated
by Evan Becker of Boxcabco,
is backlit to provide textured
lighting.

RIGHT:
In the master bath, the vanity
and stool were custom designed
to fit the wife's proportions,
allowing her to comfortably age
in place. Custom stool by Aidlin
Darling Design.

OVERLEAF:
Operable fins on the guest
bedroom window provide
privacy when closed and turn
the small room into a lantern
overlooking the pool when
opened at night.

Ridgeview House

"There was only one place a house would logically go and that place had natural constraints, including a really interesting rock formation that we wanted to preserve."
— JIM ZACK

For a couple working in the tech industry in Seattle and the Bay Area, it wasn't obvious where they should establish a weekend home, much less where they might ultimately settle. They considered destinations around the world, but for proximity, practicality and lifestyle, they kept coming back to the wine country.

"We both really enjoy food and wine and we'd been coming up and staying in hotels for long weekends and vacations," explains owner Mike Neil. "One of the things that grew on us is that it's very much an agrarian culture here. There's a connection to the land. I grew up in Michigan and my dad had a farm for a while, so it kind of clicked for us."

Neil was looking at listings online when he saw an undeveloped property on the eastern ridge of Napa Valley's Vaca Range above the town of St. Helena. All it took was one visit. "The property had no home and no infrastructure," he recalls, "but when I walked up the hill and saw the view and the big pile of rocks, that sealed the deal."

It was the owner's Seattle architect who introduced him to Zack | de Vito Architecture, with Fairweather & Associates and Randy Thueme Design joining the team as contractor and landscape architect. Neil knew he wanted a modern-leaning design, and his engineering background served him well when he showed up to initial meetings bearing lengthy documents with room-by-room specifications. The first order of business—obtaining permits—took longer than expected. The team had to satisfy county regulations about ridgetop construction and visibility from the valley below. They were also required to mitigate fire danger, which included designing a fire-engine turnaround and creating adequate water storage. They dug a well, installed a pool and used materials such as board-formed concrete, Cor-ten steel paneling and steel I-beams to meet or exceed the fire stipulations.

Given all these considerations, siting was somewhat straightforward, explains architect Jim Zack. "Ridgeview is an eight-acre site on top of a hill, but there was only one place a house would logically go and that place had natural constraints, including a really interesting rock formation that we wanted to preserve."

The west-to-southwest-facing residence aligns with the ridgeline. The structure rises above the parking level, with the formal entry to the side of the house accessed by an exterior staircase sheltered by a narrow projecting

RIGHT:
Perched on a ridge above
the town of St. Helena, a
house designed by Zack | de
Vito Architecture and built
by Fairweather & Associates
nestles between dramatic rock
outcroppings and existing
trees. The living spaces face
out over the valley while the
bedrooms enjoy more intimate
views. Custom details abound
throughout the house, as in the
front and back doors, designed
by Zack | de Vito and built by
Fairweather & Associates, and the
built-in bed and integrated side
tables in the master bedroom.
Both hot tub and pool are mere
steps from the master suite.

OVERLEAF:
The main volume, clad in cedar,
has a roof that cantilevers out
toward the view, creating a
covered outdoor entertaining
space with a full dining table,
built-in cooking facilities,
including a wood-fired oven,
and an island with waterfall
countertop.

The home's central organizing principle is its striking steel, wood and glass staircase—a sculptural presence that also carries light throughout all three levels. The owner wanted the pool right up against the house. This creates a wonderful play of light on and in the building while also providing natural cooling. Contemporary furnishings in neutral tones allow the focus to remain on the views.

overhang. The main cedar-clad volume housing the living areas protrudes into the void over the garage and faces the view on the adjacent side. There, an expressive steel-beamed overhang creates an all-season outdoor living area. Cooking and food-prep facilities with a grill, wood-burning pizza oven, and large island with waterfall countertop, a dining table for twelve, and a lounge setup with a fire feature relate to the corresponding areas within the house and more than double the living space.

The private portion of the house is demarcated by a central stairwell, beyond which lie bedrooms on two levels. The staircase is the interior's most dramatic moment, a dynamic form with wood treads spaced along steel I-beam stringers behind a glass wall. Located in the center of the house, it injects energy into the public spaces and acts as an organizing principle that ties the three levels together. "The steel with wood has a masculine look and creates a presence, yet has an open feel," says architect Lise de Vito. "Because it stretches from the upper level it pulls light down to the mudroom and wine room. It's literally a zigzag, so you see the ascension of the stairs and can peek upstairs. It also creates a sculptural element upon entry and expands the room in a very dramatic way."

The bedrooms, in contrast, are places of repose. On the ground level, the owners' suite has sliding glass doors that open to the lap pool on one side and to a private deck with hot tub backed by the rock formation on the other. Two upstairs bedrooms—accessed through a light-filled work space which has its own balcony carved out from the copper-clad volume of the house—share a deck covered by a steel-framed translucent canopy. From their perch aloft, guests are afforded a bird's-eye view over the Napa Valley.

The home is decidedly modern in form with ample amounts of steel, glass and concrete. This is balanced by cedar and Cor-ten steel—applied in large panels on the driveway side of the deck enclosure, as well as on the exterior of the private volume of the house—which injects warmth, texture and patina into the design.

De Vito along with Zack | de Vito's resident interior designer Sara Nicolas and lighting designer Sherry Weller worked closely with the owner to execute the home's many custom features, from steel elements and fixed surfaces to fabrics, lighting and such details as sapele kitchen cabinetry and eucalyptus bedroom flooring. Custom steel and walnut pieces designed by de Vito include beds, the desk and side credenza in the upstairs study, and the dining table and credenza in the great room. High-efficiency energy systems powered by photovoltaics are managed through smart home technology, while naturalistic plantings within the existing landscape of manzanita and oak contribute to the minimalist, nature-intensive feel. Whether a weekend retreat or full-time residence, this is a home that balances form and function while making the most of an incomparable climate and setting.

LEFT:
Quartz countertops define the cooking area at one end of the great room, while a custom steel and wood live-edge dining table grounds the airy space. Steel beams define the volumes and extend from inside to out. Wine storage is presented as art.

OVERLEAF:
The bedroom volume and main facade is sheathed in Cor-ten weathering steel, which naturally patinas to a rich red. A small, recessed deck outside an office area on the upper level perches over the pool below.

Sunrise Pavilion

"They wanted a very natural palette and they didn't want art; they wanted the house to be about the materiality of the architecture." — SUSAN COLLINS WEIR

This remarkable wine country property had almost everything: a scenic forty-five-minute approach up a rural winding road, a beautiful, utterly private site with far-reaching views, established olive trees and lavender beds, an orchard and vegetable gardens, a rustic modern guesthouse, and a spectacular lap pool with an adjacent trellis structure. It was all set up for the most sublime outdoors-oriented wine country lifestyle. But there was a missing piece. The property lacked a residence that tied all the elements together.

"It is a gorgeous site with a modernist cabin and large pool," explains architect Jonathan Feldman, of San Francisco-based Feldman Architecture. "But the original owners had sold before they built a main house. The new owners were fortunate to inherit something we respected, but by itself the cabin was awkward. It needed something else to relate to it."

The existing structure, a concrete and wood building with a shed roof of corrugated metal, was simple in form and set to the side of the pool. Although the detailing lacked refinement, the house had charm and was appropriate to the setting. The challenge lay in how to create a main home that would take its design cues from the guesthouse but express itself with a greater level of precision and refinement.

The buyers were design aficionados who had a clear vision for the new home. They imagined an expression of original regional modernism that would be rich in warmth and materiality. Working collaboratively, the owners and architects agreed to begin by echoing the simple shed form and aluminum doors of the existing structure. The new residence presents as modest and remarkably simple; it is a pristine, clean-lined, two-story volume with minimal detailing and furnishings. On the facade, it opens completely to the view, while from the private master bedroom, the prospect is into the Zen-like hillside garden. The lower level is mostly comprised of one expansive volume that opens to the outdoors along its entire length, stepping out onto a full-length patio then down to the pool. The central kitchen (its service area tucked out of sight behind a wall toward the hillside) is flanked by dining and seating areas. Throughout the home, the tone is restrained: a palette of grays (found both in stucco and poured-in-place concrete), and white, with Douglas fir paneling. Upstairs, the Douglas fir is repeated in the flooring. "This was a tricky project, yet so simple," says the architect, who credits contractors Cello & Maudru for

their attention to detail. "It's in the precision and minimalism of detailing where the hard work goes."

The home's furnishings and art are equally minimal. The owners, explains designer Susan Collins Weir, are passionate gardeners. For them, she said, "It was all about how to bring the landscape to the interior of the house. In our conversations, we mostly talked about the landscape, and changes to the garden over the course of the year. They wanted a very natural palette and they didn't want art; they wanted the house to be about the materiality of the architecture."

Key pieces—such as a spectacular live-edge dining table and, in the living area, a custom wool rug and steel-and-wood coffee table—were designed specifically for each space, while natural materials such as leather slingback chairs and wool and linen upholstery were used throughout the rooms. In the upstairs guest room and office, an artisan-made wood slab desk within a poured-in-place concrete form cantilevers out into the space. The effect throughout the home, says Weir, speaks to a wine country ethos: simple, organic and materially rich.

When landscape designer Gretchen Whittier of Arterra Landscape Architects was brought in to help the new building integrate into the landscape and harmonize with existing features, she found that the site was not only beautiful, but lush with madrone, manzanita, and beech. She credits the owners for their extensive knowledge of plants and their familiarity with the site. Together they chose naturalistic plantings and a mixture of wood and gravel to help the two buildings integrate into the site. Both buildings have their backs to the hillside, not just for minimal impact on the landscape but for solar management. "There's incredible light all day," Whittier says. "There's dappled morning light, then full sun, which is beautiful. And in the afternoon, when the sun goes behind the hill, it's magical. It's a hot site, but there's this large body of water in its center; even if the temperature is high, the site doesn't feel too hot."

The new building relates to the old stylistically and speaks to the pool and the view in both placement and orientation. With owner, architect, designer, and landscape architect working in concert to tread lightly, respect the site, and enhance existing features, the result is sensitive and cohesive, as well as programmatically successful. "The placement of the new building, along with the terracing and the gardens, created a holistic master plan," says the architect. "And that tied everything together."

OPPOSITE ABOVE:
The facade of the house is made entirely of sliding glass panels by Panoramah. Naturalistic plantings by Arterra Landscape Architects help the home integrate with its site.

OPPOSITE BELOW:
Interior designer Susan Collins Weir worked to achieve an airy minimalism throughout both levels of the home. A sculptural Blu Bathworks tub with a Dornbracht faucet invites one to relax and enjoy the expansive views to the south. The porcelain tile floor gives way to teak slats in the open shower area.

ABOVE:
Bleached Douglas fir paneling and polished concrete floors set the tone for the space, whose neutral colors keep the focus on the outdoors. A concrete and blackened steel fireplace anchors one end of the room, a dark wall and built-in serving area the other. Furnishings include a live-edge dining table of reclaimed Claro walnut and a blackened steel coffee table from Arborica. The architecture is dynamically expressed in the exposed-steel structure that supports the house.

Forest Aerie

"This house is full of soul." — Juancarlos Fernandez

This is a story of a magical property and uncommon relationships. It is also a tale about the soul of a place, and how a house can become the physical manifestation of that soul, bringing joy to its owners and design team in equal measure to the love and care they put into creating it.

The owners, a husband and wife from Southern California, had searched for the perfect home in the Napa Valley for three years before discovering their exceptional site. Set high in the hills of the upper Napa Valley, the forested parcel is filled with boulders, pines and oaks, with a glimpse of vineyards in the distance. The forty-acre site is graced with layered views and four miles of walking trails, which the owners stroll regularly.

Until they discovered this site, the owners were uncertain whether they would buy an existing home or build one. But if they were to build, they knew they wanted Juancarlos Fernandez, cofounder of Signum Architecture in St. Helena, to design it. Unsure whether the architect could fit the project into his schedule, they invited him to come walk the site. When Juancarlos arrived, the look in his eye told the owners all they needed to know. The site's magic affected him as well.

Early in the process Juancarlos recommended interior designers Shawback Design, while the owners brought on board landscape architect Jack Chandler, cementing a team that would work in sync through several years of design and construction. For Jack, a local legend who would pass away as the project neared completion, this project became his swan song.

The team began by trimming back the pines to expose the oaks and boulders. A single, majestic live oak that now occupies the central courtyard became the home's organizing principle, and a symbol of its relationship to the site. The structure comprises two pavilions linked by a glassed-in breezeway, which Juancarlos envisioned as a lantern in the forest. The breezeway showcases the views of the valley across the infinity pool while protecting the courtyard from the heat and wind from the west.

Wrapped in glass, the house is incredibly transparent, ushering in views of nature from every angle. This is a large house, yet the pavilions allow a real sense of privacy and the house feels intimate. "You can stand anywhere in the valley below," says Juancarlos, "and you can't see the house." The owner calls his house "an homage to what was there before us."

PREVIOUS OVERLEAF:
To create a house that lives up to the unique character of its
astounding site, the owners brought together a close-knit group
led by Juancarlos Fernandez, Partner at Signum Architecture. In
a deeply collaborative process, design decisions were made over
long lunches, and the result is a home that resounds with emotion.

ABOVE:
Anchored by a single majestic oak, the courtyard acts as the organizing principle for the design. For landscape architect Jack Chandler, a local legend who would pass away as the project neared completion, the home was his swan song.

OVERLEAF:
Set within a forested site with deeply layered views, the home cannot be seen from anywhere in the valley below.

OPPOSITE ABOVE:
The rustic finish of the stone walls provides a counterpoint to the clean lines of the floating cabinet and an Oberon pendant by Fuse Lighting.

OPPOSITE BELOW:
The master bedroom feels as if it is floating amidst the trees. A Lohja Single chandelier by Cameron Design House hangs above a custom headboard from Kroll Furniture.

ABOVE:
The team used the same stone, mined and hand-chosen from a single quarry in Italy, throughout the house, in finishes varying from polished to highly rusticated.

Throughout the house, clerestory windows bathe the interiors in light. The dining room's custom steel fireplace surround was designed by landscape architect Jack Chandler. Fully upholstered Nobile Soft dining chairs from Draenert pull up to the Draenert Atlas dining table, topped by the Lohja Four chandelier by Cameron Design House. Commissioned artwork by Brigitte McReynolds is designed to reflect the seasons.

Inside the main pavilion, a single, three-level space—cantilevered over the hillside—merges living dining and kitchen areas into a welcoming gathering place for family and friends, with his and her offices, and guest quarters tucked below on a lower level. Huge doors slide back, opening an entire wall of the kitchen to the courtyard, which, filled with the sounds of nature and water from a fountain custom-designed by Jack, is perfect for entertaining.

The second pavilion houses the couple's private spaces: a master suite, as well as rooms for exercise and meditation. The master bedroom—transparent on two sides and tucked into the hill, entirely surrounded by trees—feels like a secret tree house. From the master bedroom and bath, there isn't another building to be seen anywhere.

Visual simplicity was the key to creating the serene environment, and every detail was carefully considered. To extend the views and create a sense of balance, Juancarlos meticulously aligned openings and designed seamless and orderly connections between spaces (three stairs separate the lower living room from the dining room, and another three steps connect the dining room to the adjacent kitchen). Details are spare and materials are carefully edited. The team used the same stone, mined from a single quarry in Italy, throughout the house, in finishes varying from polished to highly rusticated. The kitchen cabinet system by Bulthaup is free from hardware and disappears when not in use.

The furnishings are quiet and restrained, an understudy to the views. "Our goal was to balance the strength of the architecture and the intense beauty of the site with interiors that had a softness about them," says Penny Shawback. Clients and designers chose furnishings jointly, even traveling to Sun Valley, Idaho, together to visit one of Penny's favorite sources.

Searching for an artistic way to create a sense of separation between the kitchen and dining room, the husband showed Penny an island that incorporated a sinuous curve. The team found a local artist to create a similar design in a soft white composite of marble and resin, its feminine curve juxtaposed with the trio of stairs that separate the two spaces. The solution, as always, lay in collaboration.

Throughout the project, decisions were made over long lunches, and deep relationships took root. "Every project has its own personality and holds its own set of values," says Penny. "This project was warm, gracious and full of trust and purpose." Juancarlos puts it simply, "This house is full of soul."

ABOVE:
Perforated steel doors slide apart, fully opening the kitchen
to the sheltered courtyard, forming a perfect space for
entertaining. When closed, the perforated panel, backlit with
light from the kitchen, washes the courtyard in a soft light.

OPPOSITE:
To separate the kitchen and dining areas, a local artist
reenvisioned a design found by the owner, using a soft
white composite of marble and resin to create the island's
sinuous curve. The kitchen cabinet system by Bulthaup, free
from hardware, disappears when not in use.

OVERLEAF:
The effect of the pavilion design is ethereal, invoking the
image of a lantern set comfortably within the forest.

Sustainable Sanctuary

"It was a fun exercise to sketch out how siting and land might shape the architecture."
— JONATHAN FELDMAN

The Santa Lucia Preserve seems a world away. Located on California's Central Coast a few miles inland from the Pacific Coast Highway, its 18,000 acres extend from sea level up to the edge of the Ventana Wilderness in the Santa Lucia Mountains and encompass parts of Monterey Canyon and the Salinas Valley. From coastal chaparral and grasslands to oak savannah and redwood forests, the preserve showcases stunning biodiversity in its botanical variety and thriving wildlife populations. It is also rich in scenic splendor. In such a place it makes perfect sense that a strong eco-consciousness would overlay thoughts on new construction. And it is a given that the community would attract those who want to tread lightly on the land in a place singularly focused on nature.

"The Santa Lucia Preserve is quite a unique development," says Brian Groza of Groza Construction. "You have a limited number of homes on very large parcels with small footprints for building, which is what makes each house so special. In the case of this house, it sits on a knoll where the undulating character of the home incorporates into the natural topography."

The Feldman Architecture-designed structure perches within the rolling hills amidst an open wildflower-studded grassland with far-reaching views of rounded hills and oak groves. It was crafted to highlight the home's connection to the land, with rammed-earth walls that gently curve with the contours of the hillside. These earthen masses—batched on-site with existing soils, decomposed granite, and some cement as a binder—play a crucial role in the home's minimal carbon footprint. Their thermal mass regulates temperatures during the heat of the day and the cool of the night and year-round through dramatic fluctuations in temperature.

The home is orientated to the south, with a large expanse of glass opening up to extend the open-plan great room to the outdoors. On one end, the roof projects to create a covered outdoor living room which faces into a grove of mature live oaks. On the south, an open patio has sunshades that can be engaged as needed. These, plus ample natural ventilation, are important players in the home's passive heating and cooling system. Integrated solar panels produce adequate energy for the home without impacting the aesthetics of its horizontal profile. Close by, three tanks for rainwater storage add visual interest while meeting the property's irrigation and fire protection needs.

The design was informed by the client's previous experience of having lived in a home designed by architect Cliff May. It was May who helped define the mid-century modern California ranch house, with its low horizontal massing, informal open-plan living and seamless integration with the outdoors. From the outset, architect Jonathan Feldman says, the approach was about blending in with the land. Rather than creating a showplace, the goal was to minimize the structure's visual impact. As the property offered multiple siting options, the process involved envisioning how each site might influence each design. "Some options were better for privacy, but others were better for views, for environmental impact or for cost," Feldman says. "It was a fun exercise to sketch out how siting and land might shape the architecture." One site quickly rose to the top of the list. There, the structure could be nestled below the top of the hill, where it would defer to the topography while still enjoying spectacular views in all directions.

The client loved the idea of curved walls, hence overlapping arcing volumes that snake between the landforms and stitch the building into the broader landscape. These are offset to allow indoor-outdoor connections and points of entry, while the extension of the curved walls into the landscape draws the eye and focuses the view. A series of curved shed roofs float above the anchoring walls, reinforcing the notion of shelter and creating the feel of a pavilion. Materiality is simple, from the rammed-earth walls, white oak cabinets, and light-toned Douglas fir ceiling, slats, and trim, to the concrete floor that flows through the house and out the doors.

A minimalist planting palette conceived by landscape architect Joni Janecki of Joni L. Janecki & Associates continues the theme of simplicity and naturalness that ties the home effortlessly to its setting. "The intrinsic beauty of this California grassland and oak savanna habitat captured our client's heart," she says, "so integrating the home into the site and blurring the edges between wild lands and tamed landscape was of utmost importance."

By working with the topography and preserving the oak and grassland habitat as much possible, the team was able to seamlessly meld the new and existing landscape. Protection of the lupine and wildflower grassland was also prioritized. To heal the site after construction, top soil was salvaged and distributed over the impacted areas and then spread with a mixture of locally collected wildflowers and grasses. Finally, interplanting lupine, California poppy and native grasses allowed the new landscape to blend with the native grassland and oak habitat.

The home was the first LEED platinum-certified home on California's Central Coast and has won multiple design awards. But its true testament lies in the homeowner's lived experience. For an avid gardener, cook and horseback rider who had long dreamt of a home immersed in nature, this compact and conscientious design allows her to celebrate the natural world while treading lightly on the land.

PREVIOUS OVERLEAF:
A house designed as a nature-intensive retirement home by Feldman Architecture perches just below a ridgeline on the 18,000-acre Santa Lucia Preserve in the Carmel Valley. Contractor Brian Groza built the rammed-earth walls, batched on-site, to contour with the hillside. The landscape plan by Joni Janecki ties the home to its setting by preserving the oak woodlands, native grassland and lupine meadows as much as possible.

OPPOSITE:
Three rainwater tanks serve a crucial role in sustainability and fire protection while adding sculptural interest. Gently curved roofs seem to float above the glassy expanses.

ABOVE:
Furnishings selected by designer Jay Jeffers—The Studio
marry the airiness of a George Nelson Bubble Lamp Saucer
with the clean lines of a 1960s Danish rosewood credenza.

ABOVE:
In the open living area, a 1953 Vladimir Kagan Contour Chair rests atop a contemporary Turkish carpet made from recycled antique Kilims.

OVERLEAF:
The house has a transparency day and night. The low profile of the 1940s bronze Walter Lamb Rocking Lounge Chairs allows for unimpeded views into the living space and kitchen. The sofa is a 1950s Edward Wormley for Dunbar, the kitchen countertops are Toscana Quartz, and the Douglas fir millwork is custom.

Downtempo

"We called the house 'Downtempo' because we felt it captured the rhythms of the house, and the goals our clients were hoping to achieve."
— JARROD DENTON

Set in an isolated valley in the Mayacamas Mountains between the valleys of Sonoma and Napa, this unique home lies just ten minutes by car from the town of Calistoga yet feels as if it were a million miles from anywhere. The owners envisioned a retreat where they could build lasting memories with their two children, entertain friends and enjoy the slower pace of life in the wine country.

Unsure whether they wanted to buy or build, the owners reached out to Jarrod Denton, cofounder of St. Helena–based Signum Architecture, to help them explore the possibilities. After visiting numerous potential building sites, they were brought to a site in Franz Valley. An avid biker, Jarrod was familiar with this hidden valley from regular bike-riding excursions in the area. Comprising two small knolls with a gentle swale in between, the building site backs up to the woodlands, with a creek running below and sweeping views in multiple directions. In one direction lay views down the valley, in the other lay views of a 3,000-acre nature preserve.

"Within this sensitive terrain, adjacent to the preserve and prone to forest fires, sustainability and fire resistance were critical," says Jarrod, "but the site was spectacular."

In order to build quickly and sustainably, Jarrod and his team designed the home using a combination of prefabricated modular units and on-site construction, working with prefab manufacturer Method Homes and local contractor Fairweather & Associates. Using eleven prefabricated modules (five downstairs and six upstairs), the team ended up with a ratio of roughly 80 percent prefab to 20 percent site-built construction. The living room (which occupies the center of the ground floor), pool, terraces and foundations were built before the modules arrived on site. After they arrived, the modules were stitched together, then custom elements—roof, utility spaces and parapets—were built in place. "The day the modules arrived was like Christmas," Jarrod says with a smile.

"We knew this project was going to encourage us to push the envelope of what we could do, both in terms of construction and delivery," says Brian Abramson, founder of Method Homes.

Working with prefabricated modules resulted in a design process that was anything but familiar, upending the decision-making process. "We were working on excavation and foundations while looking at fixtures and

finishes," says Jarrod. "It was a completely different way to approach design, but it really brought the team together."

The resulting structure is lean and bold, with a restrained palette of materials. Bands of black aluminum surround fields of clear cedar and shou sugi ban (a charred wood finish that is naturally resistant to fire). The siding is recessed within the thick perimeter borders, opening up areas for shade and balconies. Conditioned, ventless attic space, fire-resistant materials and a defensible landscape space around the home help temper fire risk.

Within the bold architectural envelope, designer Alison Damonte created an environment of what she calls "maximal minimalism." Having worked with the clients to design their primary home in urban Berkeley not far away, Alison knew her clients well. Her eclectic but highly curated interiors are a natural extension of the vibe they had created in their first project together—a nod to the earthy, textural geometric aesthetic of the 1960s and 1970s. The mix of vintage and contemporary pieces in saturated hues of blue and green mix comfortably with earthy rusts and browns, bringing personality and depth to the home. A neutral palette "just isn't me," says Alison, and it didn't fit her clients either.

She knew, for example, that the couple had come to love wall coverings in the design of their Berkeley home, so she felt comfortable suggesting bold choices for their Calistoga property. "I'm not one to shy away from a bright color or a bold pattern," she asserts. Patterns and colors are biggest and boldest in small spaces, where the couple can immerse themselves, then retire to the larger living spaces where the volume is turned down a bit. The kitchen backsplash is a perfect example: bold and geometric, the pattern stands up to the bold architectural envelope and hints of vintage vinyl records in a subtle reference to the husband's work at the intersection of music and technology. Vintage cassette wallpaper in a small bath near the media room does the same.

The clients have been building their collection of contemporary photography and video art for several decades. "I wanted to give them furniture that stood up to the art," Alison confides. Each piece of furniture is bespoke, collected and tied to the client in some way. The living room feels like a real life representation of the collage piece by Laurie Simmons (mother to actress Lena Dunham), that hangs above the long, linear fireplace. The eclectic collage the designer has created on the interior comes together with the home's gallery-like white walls to create a balanced vessel for the couple's art collection, and a perfect country escape for this highly creative family.

RIGHT:
In the living room, vintage
Brazilian Rosewood chairs and
a single chair by Pierre Paulin
surround a custom sofa facing
the open wall to the pool terrace.
A collage piece by artist Laurie
Simmons (mother to actress
Lena Dunham) hangs above
the fireplace.

OVERLEAF:
Architect Jarrod Denton pulled
the shou sugi ban finish into the
dining room to create a sense
of cohesion. A chandelier from
Lindsey Adelman hangs above an
Egg Collective dining table and
vintage chairs by Matteo Grassi;
sconces are from Chen Chen &
Kai Williams.

ABOVE:
A custom bed covered in Romo Fabric sits atop an area rug by Mark Nelson in the master bedroom. Recessing the siding within thick perimeter borders allowed the architects to create inset balconies where the owners can sit and enjoy the view.

OPPOSITE ABOVE:
Vintage cassette wallpaper by Rebel Walls in a small bath near the media room is one of numerous playful references to the husband's work at the intersection of music and technology.

OPPOSITE BELOW:
In the son's bedroom, a bed by The Inside is topped by pillows from Seven Sundays Studios. Nightstand is from Schoolhouse Electric, artwork is *Buckaroo Motel, Tucumcari, New Mexico* by Ed Freeman.

ABOVE:
Bands of black aluminum surround fields of clear cedar and shou sugi ban. The siding is recessed within the thick perimeter borders, opening up areas for shade and balconies.

RIGHT:
"From the earliest sketches, one theme that continued to play out was the horizontality of the structure, and the simplicity of working with just three exterior materials," says architect Jarrod Denton.

Recreation
& Renewal

Zinfandel Barn

"This is a place to entertain and live the lifestyle, with warm weather and beautiful views, out in the country." — PENNY SHAWBACK

A vintage barn and ancient oak tree provided the inspiration and design cues for a mid Napa Valley estate set amidst Zinfandel vines. The oak served as the site plan's organizing principle, the barn the form for a new structure that would serve as guesthouse, gathering spot, and destination. Designer Penny Shawback of Shawback Design assembled a team—Field Architecture, Grassi & Associates contracting, and Surfacedesign landscape architects—to craft a wine country idyll comprised of a main house, garage, pool, tennis court, firepit and barn. The historic barn was reclaimed for furniture and other uses, while its form was extended to house the vintage tractor and pickup truck the owners inherited with the property.

The barn's reclaimed barnwood exterior yields to an interior executed in beams and trusses with iron connective detail (fabricated by British Columbia-based Spearhead), wire-brushed paneling, and radiant-heat concrete floors. Its double-height vaulted middle section houses a dining table (easily moved to make way for dance parties); the open sleeping loft can house a family of four. Tucked under the sloping edges are the kitchen and lounge with sectionals, ottomans and a TV. Clerestory windows flood the space with light, while refinement is conveyed in natural stone countertops in the kitchen, Heath tile and plaster walls in the bathroom, luxurious linens, and an equine painting by Nicole Charbonnet—all executed by Shawback in partnership with her son and business partner, Damon Savoia, and his wife, project manager Julie Savoia.

The studio-blown glass chandelier is undoubtedly the barn's touchstone item; it adds drama and elegance with a modern sensibility. Designed by Damon Savoia, it was this piece that sparked the founding of his custom lighting company, Longhouse. When the chandelier is illuminated at night, the barn becomes a beacon. Viewed from the house and pool—and through the house from the opposite side, where the long view lines up with the ancient oak tree—it becomes a focal point.

Whether in use or merely acting as a backdrop, the Zin Barn is central to the project's entire ethos. "This couple loves to entertain relatives and friends with lots of children," explains Shawback. "They'll set up tents on the lawn and show movies in the barn. For them this is a place to entertain and live the lifestyle, with warm weather and beautiful views, out in the country."

An iconic barn set within a Zinfandel vineyard serves as a focal point from the main house, especially when lit at night. It is also a destination, guesthouse and entertaining venue. Field Architecture's design was executed by Grassi & Associates, with Surfacedesign's landscaping plan tying the structural components together. Interior designer Penny Shawback, her son and partner Damon Savoia and Damon's wife Julie married the reclaimed barnwood exterior and beamed and trussed interior with minimal contemporary-leaning furnishings. The studio-blown glass chandelier was designed by Damon Savoia and sparked the founding of his custom lighting company, Longhouse.

Pool House in a Meadow

"With small buildings you have a small bucket. The tricky part is to put all of your design ideas into this small bucket without overcooking it."
— GEORGE BEVAN

Set on a five-acre parcel at the southern end of the Napa Valley, this small structure is composed of interior and covered exterior spaces in exactly equal measure, combining pool house and guest quarters within a single structure. Set at a distance from the client's existing home, across a grassy meadow, the pool house is an architectural departure from the main house. Though it echoes the clean lines of the client's modern home, it establishes its own distinct aesthetic within the meadow.

George Bevan, principal of Sonoma-based architectural firm Bevan & Associates, collaborated with Mike Lucas, partner at Healdsburg-based landscape architecture firm Lucas & Lucas, whom he has known since graduate school. The result is a symbiotic relationship between architecture and landscape.

The building's low-slung profile opens up to the landscape, without detracting from the serenity of the home's views of the meadow. George describes it as "a sliver, or a shard, of a building within nature." Just a peak of the structure is visible through the varied carpet of native grasses.

The asymmetrical butterfly roof effectively delineates the building's dual uses, with public entertaining spaces housed under the roofline's primary angle, and private guest quarters tucked under the smaller secondary section. The roof extends far beyond the building footprint to form a roomy outdoor dining area on one side and a comfortable seating area for guests at the outdoor kitchen on the other.

Restraint was critical to the design. Exterior walls, roof and trellises are carried out in a uniformly dark shade, allowing the white interior walls and undersides of the extruded roofline—clad in wood—to pop. "With small buildings you have a small bucket," says George. "The tricky part is to put all of your design ideas into this small bucket without overcooking it."

Set in the lower Napa Valley close to downtown Napa, this retreat, which is set at a distance from the property's main house, combines pool house and guest quarters in a single building. This contemporary sliver of a building with its distinctive butterfly roof, designed by George Bevan, Principal of Bevan + Associates, is tucked into a varied meadow of native grasses designed by Mike Lucas, Principal of Lucas & Lucas Landscape Architecture.

Garden to Table

"There's a balance of formality and casualness, with a real rigor in that it feels casual but is grounded in its place in the landscape." — ANDREW MANN

A weekend retreat in Sonoma County for a dual-career couple with young children had at its heart a desire to connect with the landscape through food and cooking. An existing home with pool, pool house, vineyards and an orchard was the starting point for a project that modernized the 1970s-era dwellings, integrated them more fully with the outdoors and celebrated the property's garden-to-table ethos with a new open-air kitchen, dining and potting shed pavilion.

Built on the site of an old arbor set within a fruit orchard a short distance from the house, the simple shed-roof volume opens out toward curvilinear raised beds and cutting gardens which are terraced into the sloping hillside below. Architect Andrew Mann, landscape designer Christa Moné and Sawyer Construction worked closely with the owners to conceive its materiality, functionality and form. Western red cedar, poured concrete floors, a full kitchen with appliances and a pizza oven, and walk-in spaces for cooking gear and gardening tools tucked behind sliding barn doors are set within a structure that references the region's agricultural heritage.

The pavilion serves as an on-property destination for family meals and entertaining, and for the homeowners, who are ardent gardeners and cooks. Twice a year, Moné collaborates with the clients to refresh cut flower beds designed by theme and to update production gardens with a changing array of vegetables such as broccolini, eggplant and Lacinato kale. "Each bed is purposefully designed to be productive and drop-dead gorgeous," she says. Special touches include an espaliered tomato patch cultivated to climb up hog wire panels and dwarf citrus containers filled with herbs.

The pavilion and garden are perfectly integrated into the pastoral site. Explains architect Andrew Mann, "It's designed to be formal in plan while working with existing contours to create defined spaces. There's a balance of formality and casualness, with a real rigor in that it feels casual but is grounded in its place in the landscape. It's very much about California living and the quality of life."

For a young family seeking to connect to the land through cooking and gardening, architect Andrew Mann created an open-air pavilion with wood-fired oven, cooking facilities and a built-in potting shed. Christa Moné designed the garden, which she updates twice a year. The owners chose the furnishings for the space, including Room & Board's cheerful Caprice chairs and a custom table.

Inside-Outside Barn

"The project is as much a piece of art as it is a piece of architecture.
It's all about light." — WILLIAM DUFF

"The project is as much a piece of art as it is a piece of architecture," says William Duff, founder of William Duff Architects. "It's about light—what the light does throughout the day, and how artificial light illuminates the building after dark."

The clients for this project are avid art collectors from Dallas who spend their summers in Napa Valley. They wanted to build a space for entertaining and thought they might use the barn, but they weren't sure the dilapidated structure was worth saving. William Duff and his team walked through the building, noticed how the light was cast into the interior through the slatted boards (which had shrunk over time to allow the light through), and immediately began to conjure ways to turn the building into a study of light.

Keeping the shell intact, the team modified it to capture and play with the light. "The barn was pretty ramshackle when we started," says principal Jim Westover. The finished product comprises two free-standing rectangular volumes set within the seismically reinforced shell of the barn, covered entirely in reflective surfaces. At night, the light bounces off the surfaces, illuminating the barn like a lantern. The team worked with lighting expert Eric Johnson, essentially sculpting the space with light.

Mirrored walls line the central dining space. A one-way mirror allows the occupants of the adjacent exercise room to see the vineyards while obscuring them from view on the exterior. The small building—lifted three steps above grade to accommodate views over the surrounding vineyards—feels like an island in the landscape. The mirrored central space allows visitors to feel like they are inside and outside the building at the same time.

This small building, which at first glance is a purely historic element of the landscape, is also a simply wrought play on light and the ways that architecture can create an experience of place.

Set amidst the vineyards on the valley floor, this small building turns a study of light and shadow into a magical pavilion for entertaining within the stunning landscape of the wine country. At once historic and contemporary, inside and outside, rustic and sophisticated, it is a quintessential example of wine country design at its best.

The
Teams

AGRARIAN SPIRIT

Vineyard's Edge, CALISTOGA

Architecture: WADE DESIGN ARCHITECTS
Interior Design: GEREMIA DESIGN
Landscape Design: GROUND STUDIO LANDSCAPE
    ARCHITECTURE
Construction: TOTAL CONCEPTS
Photography: SUZANNA SCOTT PHOTOGRAPHY

Modern Agrarian, RUTHERFORD

Architecture: PFAU LONG ARCHITECTURE
Interior Design: PFAU LONG ARCHITECTURE
Landscape Design: LUTSKO ASSOCIATES
Construction: GRASSI & ASSOCIATES
Photography: ART GRAY PHOTOGRAPHY

Woodland Farmhouse, VALLEY OF THE MOON, SONOMA

Architecture: NICHOLAS LEE ARCHITECTS
Design: ROSSI SCOTT
Construction: EAMES CONSTRUCTION
Photography: ADAM POTTS PHOTOGRAPHY

Rustic Estate, CALISTOGA

Architecture: AMY A. ALPER, ARCHITECT
Interior Design: JENNIFER ROBIN INTERIORS
Landscape Design: MERGE STUDIO, INC.
Construction: TOTAL CONCEPTS
Photography: JOHN MERKL PHOTOGRAPHY

Nestled in Nature, SONOMA

Architecture: MICHAEL GUTHRIE & COMPANY ARCHITECTS
Interior Design: JEFF SCHLARB DESIGN STUDIO
Landscape Design: ROCHE + ROCHE LANDSCAPE
    ARCHITECTURE
Construction: REITER FINE HOME BUILDING
Photography: AUBRIE PICK PHOTOGRAPHY, MARION
    BRENNER PHOTOGRAPHY

Refined Farmhouse, CALISTOGA

Architecture: POLSKY PERLSTEIN ARCHITECTS
Interior Design: PAULINA PERRAULT INTERIORS
Landscape Design: LUCAS & LUCAS LANDSCAPE
    ARCHITECTURE; OWNERS
Construction: ARMADA BUILDERS & INTERIORS
Photography: LAURA REOCH, SEPTEMBER-DAYS
    PHOTOGRAPHY

A Cottage Reborn, CALISTOGA

Architecture: BOHLIN CYWINSKI JACKSON
Interior design: BOHLIN CYWINSKI JACKSON
Landscape Design: EINWILLERKUEHL LANDSCAPE
    ARCHITECTURE
Construction: FAIRWEATHER & ASSOCIATES
Photography: MATTHEW MILLMAN PHOTOGRAPHY

Historic Meets Modern, SONOMA

Architecture: WADE DESIGN ARCHITECTS
Interior Design: JENNIFER ROBIN INTERIORS
Landscape Design: ROZANSKI DESIGN
Construction: EARTHTONE CONSTRUCTION
Photography: PAUL DYER PHOTOGRAPHY

The Bird House, OAKVILLE

Architecture: JACOBSEN ARCHITECTURE
Interior Design: JEFF ATLAS (OWNER)
Landscape Design: TERRE FERMA LANDSCAPES
Construction: CENTRIC GENERAL CONTRACTORS
Photography: ADAM POTTS PHOTOGRAPHY, DOUGLAS
    STERLING PHOTOGRAPHY

WINE COUNTRY CONTEMPORARY

Black Box House, LOVALL VALLEY

Architecture: BEVAN & ASSOCIATES
Interior Design: BEVAN & ASSOCIATES; OWNER
Landscape Design: LUCAS & LUCAS LANDSCAPE
    ARCHITECTURE
Construction: TRAINOR BUILDERS
Photography: DOUGLAS FRIEDMAN PHOTOGRAPHY

Vintner's View, DRY CREEK VALLEY

Architecture: SUTRO ARCHITECTS
Interior Design: ADEENI DESIGN GROUP
Landscape Design: ARTERRA LANDSCAPE ARCHITECTS
Construction: UPSCALE CONSTRUCTION
Photography: CHRISTOPHER STARK PHOTOGRAPHY

Winged Retreat, CARMEL VALLEY

Architecture: AIDLIN DARLING DESIGN
Interior Design: MCBRIDE DESIGN
Landscape Design: GROUND STUDIO LANDSCAPE
    ARCHITECTURE
Construction: CARROLL & STRONG BUILDERS
Photography: MATTHEW MILLMAN PHOTOGRAPHY

Ridgeview House, VACA MOUNTAINS

Architecture: ZACK | DE VITO ARCHITECTURE +
    CONSTRUCTION
Interior Design: ZACK | DE VITO ARCHITECTURE +
    CONSTRUCTION, OWNER
Landscape Design: RANDY THUEME DESIGN
Construction: FAIRWEATHER & ASSOCIATES
Photography: CESAR RUBIO PHOTOGRAPHY

Sunrise Pavilion, RUSSIAN RIVER VALLEY

Architecture: FELDMAN ARCHITECTURE
Interior Design: STUDIO COLLINS WEIR
Landscape Design: ARTERRA LANDSCAPE ARCHITECTS
Construction: CELLO & MAUDRU CONSTRUCTION
Photography: ADAM ROUSE PHOTOGRAPHY

Forest Aerie, HOWELL MOUNTAIN

Architecture: SIGNUM ARCHITECTURE
Interior Design: SHAWBACK DESIGN
Landscape Design: JACK CHANDLER DESIGN
Construction: CELLO & MAUDRU CONSTRUCTION
Photography: ADAM ROUSE PHOTOGRAPHY

Sustainable Sanctuary, CARMEL VALLEY

Architecture: FELDMAN ARCHITECTURE
Interior Design: JAY JEFFERS—THE STUDIO
Landscape Design: JONI L. JANECKI + ASSOCIATES
Construction: GROZA CONSTRUCTION
Photography: JOE FLETCHER PHOTOGRAPHY

Downtempo, FRANZ VALLEY

Architecture: SIGNUM ARCHITECTURE
Interior Design: ALISON DAMONTE DESIGN
Landscape Design: TERREMOTO
Construction: METHOD HOMES; FAIRWEATHER & ASSOCIATES
Photography: BRUCE DAMONTE PHOTOGRAPHY

RECREATION & RENEWAL

Zinfandel Barn, OAK KNOLL DISTRICT

Architecture: FIELD ARCHITECTURE
Interior Design: SHAWBACK DESIGN
Landscape Design: SURFACEDESIGN
Construction: GRASSI & ASSOCIATES
Photography: MATTHEW MILLMAN PHOTOGRAPHY

Pool House in a Meadow, VICHY DISTRICT, NAPA

Architecture: BEVAN & ASSOCIATES
Landscape Design: LUCAS & LUCAS LANDSCAPE
    ARCHITECTURE
Construction: TRAINOR BUILDERS
Photography: ERIC RORER PHOTOGRAPHY

Garden to Table, SONOMA

Architecture: ANDREW MANN ARCHITECTURE
Garden Design: CHRISTA MONÉ
Construction: SAWYER CONSTRUCTION
Photography: DAVID WAKELY PHOTOGRAPHY

Inside-Outside Barn, NAPA

Architecture: WILLIAM DUFF ARCHITECTS
Interior Design: ROBERT WILLIAM DAILEY DESIGN &
    DECORATION
Landscape Design: STEVEN ARNS, LANDSCAPE ARCHITECT
Construction: CENTRIC GENERAL CONTRACTORS
Photography: MATTHEW MILLMAN PHOTOGRAPHY